The Passionate Gardener

DES KENNEDY

ADVENTURES *of an*
ARDENT GREEN THUMB

THE PASSIONATE GARDENER

GREYSTONE BOOKS

Douglas & McIntyre Publishing Group

Vancouver/Toronto/Berkeley

Greystone Books
A division of Douglas & McIntyre Ltd.
2323 Quebec Street, Suite 201
Vancouver, British Columbia
Canada v5T 4S7
www.greystonebooks.com

Library and Archives Canada Cataloguing in Publication
Kennedy, Des
The passionate gardener : adventures of an ardent green
thumb / Des Kennedy.
ISBN-13: 978-1-55365-198-7 ·ISBN-10: 1-55365-198-7
1. Gardening—Humor. 2. Gardening—Anecdotes. I. Title.
SB455.K465 2006   635.02′07   C2006-903496-6

Cover and text design by Naomi MacDougall
Cover photograph of Des Kennedy by Sandy Kennedy

Portions of several chapters in this book appeared in different
form in *Gardening Life* and *GardenWise* magazines

Printed and bound in Canada by Friesens
Printed on acid-free paper that is forest friendly
(100% post-consumer recycled paper) and has been processed chlorine free.
Distributed in the U.S. by Publishers Group West

We gratefully acknowledge the financial support of the Canada Council for
the Arts, the British Columbia Arts Council, and the Government of Canada
through the Book Publishing Industry Development Program (BPIDP) for our
publishing activities.

For Sandy

W E WILL ENDEAVOUR to shew how the aire and genious of Gardens operat upon humane spirits towards virtue and sanctitie, I meane in a remote, preparatory and instrumentall working. How Caves, Grotts, Mounts, and irregular ornaments of Gardens do contribute to contemplative and philosophicall Enthusiasms; how Elysium, Antrum, Nemus, Paradysus, Hortus, Lucus, &c., signifie all of them rem sacram et divinam; for these expedients do influence the soule and spirits of man, and prepare them for converse with good Angells; besides which, they contribute to the lesse abstracted pleasures, phylosophy naturall and longevitie.

—*John Evelyn in a letter to Sir Thomas Browne, 1657*

Contents

Introduction

THE GREAT CZECH writer Karel Capek put it bluntly: "Let no one think that real gardening is a bucolic and meditative occupation. It is an insatiable passion, like everything else to which a man gives his heart." Those who have given their heart to a garden—or had their heart stolen by it, more likely—know full well how insatiable is the passion to which they've succumbed.

Less clear is how and why gardening so thoroughly captivates us. My own first venture into the garden was not especially promising. For reasons known only to the genius of childhood, I went out one fine day and methodically cut down a whole bed of blooming flowers—chrysanthemums, I think—in my parents' garden. We lived those days in a stone cottage on the grounds of a convent school for girls in Woolton Village, Merseyside, a suburb of

Liverpool. My father was the farm bailiff, responsible for the crops and animals that supplied the convent's kitchen. Nuns move like imposing black ghosts through my dim early memories.

I have a faded photograph of myself as a fair-haired little fellow in short pants standing in a field of cut grass, with fences and large deciduous trees in the background. A hill rises behind me—I believe this is Beacon Hill, where signal fires were lit in ancient times. The scent of new-mown hay, the chittering of songbirds in hedgerows, the sight of the moon shining above Beacon Hill touched my childhood soul in a way I would not understand for decades. A passion to garden may have been clandestinely seeded there.

When I was ten years old, the family emigrated from England to Canada, settling in Weston, a suburb of Toronto. This move was ostensibly motivated by my parents' desire to provide my brothers and me with better opportunities than those offered to working-class kids in postwar England. I suspect the urge to acquire some land of their own on which to garden was at least a contributing factor in the decision, and within a year our little city lot was chockablock with flowers and vegetables.

By the age of sixteen I'd become convinced that I had a religious vocation, had been singled out and called by God Himself to become a priest. The conviction was sufficiently strong that I devoted eight long years to living in monastic seminaries operated by the Passionist Fathers, whose motto was: "May the Passion of Jesus Christ be ever in our hearts." Unlike the Trappists and some other monastic orders, the Passionists were indifferent to horticulture, and so the seed continued to lie dormant.

During the latter days of my monastic seclusion, I began imagining myself to be a poet. This diversion may have started innocently enough with reading Gerard Manley Hopkins and John Donne, but it soon embraced William Carlos Williams, Allen Ginsberg, and others of their ilk. Assigned to a monastery in New York City, I fell in with a gang of irreligious poets in the East Village and got swept up in the civil rights/anti–Vietnam War/Woodstock maelstrom of those turbulent times. Radical politics and poetry were not at all what the Passionists had in mind, and I was defrocked before I was properly frocked.

Cast loose, I started over in Vancouver, on Canada's west coast, trying my hand first at teaching high school and then at working with street kids. There I met an entrancing social worker who was fated to become my life companion. In the flush of young love, I was blissfully unaware that she might be one of Flora's enchantresses, sent to lead me by gentle measures back to the garden. Scarcely had our marriage vows been pledged, now thirty-five years ago, than we were on our way out of the city to begin life together on eleven acres of mostly conifer forest on one of British Columbia's fabled Gulf Islands.

Although we planned from the outset to grow our own fruits and vegetables—along with keeping goats, chickens, ducks, geese, and rabbits—this lifestyle change was to my mind a venture into not so much serious gardening as enlightened husbandry. I imagined living a simple, frugal, tranquil existence, occasionally laboring at a leisurely pace that afforded an abundance of time to get on with my writing.

What in fact occurred was the biographical equivalent of the persistent winter rains that make possible the lush growth of the coastal temperate rain forest. After we built a little house from recycled and hand-hewn materials and were more or less settled, gardening burst into our lives like a howling southeaster. It became for us, as for so many others, Capek's insatiable passion, completely circumscribing how we live. Nowadays, we maintain a large fruit and vegetable garden that supplies much of our food throughout the year. An even larger ornamental garden, about twenty years old, rises in terraced levels in front of the house. Its early character of massed blooming annuals, biennials, and perennials has gradually given way to a more textured, all-season garden of trees, shrubs, grasses, and hardy perennials. Native and wildlife-friendly plants help stitch the garden into the surrounding woodlands, as do using native stone and cedar in our hardscape and designing beds that curve and flow the way the forest landscape does. We are neither great nor expert gardeners. We muddle along, make mistakes, and muddle some more.

Not content with laying claim to our afternoons outdoors, gardening soon pushed its way into the small study where I spend my mornings writing. After I published a first book on natural history, a cunning publisher beguiled me into writing a gardening book. Before I fully realized what was happening, I found myself writing a gardening column for a national newspaper, contributing gardening bits to a national television program, giving speeches at prestigious gatherings of gardeners, and leading garden tours overseas. Certain misguided persons started referring to me as a "gardening guru." It was preposterous. My entire life had been hijacked by gardening.

But what a happy hijacking. Living comfortably below the poverty level and content to do better with less, my companion, Sandy, and I are free to work in the gardens, orchard, and woodlands. Not exclusively, of course— there's always something or other going on in the community or in the political affairs of the region—but working on the property forms the backbone of our days. It is a seasonal life, an engagement with plants and creatures, stone and soil, winds and frosts, that I would not trade for another.

There is a bedrock wisdom to this earthy vocation, for the garden is a work of lifelong education. Gardeners learn to appreciate the subtle interactions among plants, their mysterious ways of accommodating and influencing one another. We come to accept that certain plants, like certain people, die before their time through no fault of ours. With each fragmentary insight we grow a little more confident, a little less prone to berate ourselves when something goes wrong. Most importantly, we learn to cherish those multiple small moments of perfection that every garden offers. The wisdom gained over time instructs us how little we really know of all there is to know about gardening and its relationship both to the rest of nature and to the human spirit.

An infatuation with Flora, goddess of flowers, is by its nature a perpetually unfinished affair. Creating a garden is not the same as writing a novel or chiseling a sculpture, because the garden is never complete. It may be abandoned, it may be demolished, but so long as it exists it continues to evolve into something new, all the while retaining a splendid cyclical continuity. The tumult of spring and the melancholy of autumn are at least as poignant after thirty years of gardening as they were in those first, tentative years. The chilly brilliance of snowdrops in late winter plucks a chord within us as sweetly now as the first time we experienced it. The luckiest among us drift into old age within the garden. Bones, muscles, and sinews may begin to complain, but the passion's still there: so much still to do, so many possibilities still to explore.

Steeped in the lessons of seasonal living, gardeners know all too well how brief the flight of life really is. Our allotted portion of gaiety, of joy, is sufficiently small we do well to squander none of it. So laughter rings through the garden as we delight in our creations and chuckle at our follies. Ours is a luxury not enjoyed by a huge percentage of the planet's population. Recognizing that our sanctuaries are places of privilege, many of us feel some ambivalence about rejoicing in a beneficence denied to so many others and, it must be said, in part made possible by their exploitation. And yet, without beauty and laughter, where would we be? As Virginia Woolf wrote: "The beauty of the world . . . has two edges, one of laughter, one of anguish, cutting the heart asunder." Both are among the fruits of this insatiable passion. This book is by way of appreciation to gardeners everywhere who go about the vital work of sustaining a beautiful and bountiful world.

A NOTE ON PLANT NAMES

Experienced gardeners will need no explanation of the format for plant names, but new or would-be gardeners might appreciate the following explanation of the style used in this book.

COMMON NAMES: lowercase, as in baby's breath
CULTIVARS: varieties produced by cultivation are often registered trademarks and so all take capital letters, as in Wisely Pink
GENUS AND SPECIES: italics, as in *Acer hookeri*

'Tis Always the Season

THE GARDENER, BY rights, should be a contented creature in midwinter. The glories of the previous summer's garden linger in the memory as testament to one's genius. The possibilities for even higher refinements in the year ahead glitter like stars on clear cold nights. In the blessed hiatus of winter, one is free to remember and to dream. That's the hypothesis. But in the final days of January one winter, I was reminded again of how viciously gardeners who let down their guard can be blindsided in the dormant season.

We'd had a cold, steady rain all day. I'd spent the afternoon sprawled on damp earth, excavating the crawl space under our house. This is a task best undertaken before a house is built, but that's not my way of doing things. Around five in the evening I emerged from the crawl space filthy and freezing, craving a hot shower, a revivifying drink, and a comfortable dinner. Pausing in the dark before going indoors, I noticed that the rain was now mixed with flakes of wet snow. Not another bloody snowstorm! We'd had two substantial snowfalls in the previous weeks, the heaviest just before Christmas. Amply warned by weather forecasters, on each occasion we'd dutifully marched outdoors and shaken accumulating snow from vulnerable trees and shrubs, thereby averting serious breakage. Concerned that we might be seeing the beginnings of another heavy snowfall, I called the local weather station. A recorded message predicted, "Showers mixed with wet snow at higher elevations." Nothing too alarming on the horizon, obviously. Reassured, we settled down to a cozy evening indoors. Rain continued, with increasing wet snow. We stayed up for the 11 PM forecast, which called for "light snow." And off we went to bed.

We awoke to an unusually luminous light at dawn. The power was out. The yard and surrounding forest were swathed in deep snow. The place resembled a sentimental Christmas card come to life. But when we stepped outdoors, the beauty of the winter scene curdled to horror. The garden had been devastated. Our oldest *Cornus kousa*, in front of the house—a dogwood of sublime beauty when blooming in June—had lost the top of its crown, with several thick limbs snapped off. Farther on, a paperbark maple had a major limb torn from its trunk. The halesia silver bell lay flat on the ground, as did the Japanese snowbell, *Styrax japonica*. A Mount Etna broom I'd spent years training into a thirteen-foot-tall beauty had crumpled, too. A pair of European birches were weeping to the ground, just as Robert Frost described. Similarly assailed, golden and black bamboos were bowed to the earth like the heads of grieving widows. A young *Magnolia grandiflora*—whose large, evergreen leaves normally make it vulnerable to heavy snow—remained marvelously upright, a testament to my recent anti-snowfall pruning. But small consolation that was, for the beautiful little blue mimosa we'd coddled through seven previous winters now lay flattened by snowslides off the roof, its roots cruelly torn from the earth.

After such disasters one scuttles around fretting and attempting remediation. All the while the message rings clear and unequivocal in one's mind: You should have been out there last night, bozo, shaking the snow off! Without your dereliction of duty, this calamity would not have occurred. Yes, you know you should have taken the necessary precautions, but you were so weary and cold from a long day outdoors. Plus the forecasters failed to forewarn you. Yes, it was the forecaster's fault, not yours—mediocre meteorologists were to blame for this mess, not you!

The following days were spent dissecting the disaster with gardening colleagues. Of course, Ms. X had been out in her garden at midnight, shaking snow from every tree, and suffered not a twig's worth of damage. Gratifyingly, Madame Y—known far and wide as a fastidious groundskeeper—had uncharacteristically abandoned her garden

in favor of the ski hill and suffered destruction compara-
ble to our own. Sharing misery with others both amplifies
and mollifies its sting.

Catastrophe is a frequent visitor to the winter garden, but so is ecstasy. Another episode also began in the
crawl space under our house. The ill-named space is actually much too cramped for crawling. When occasionally
required to enter it, I have to flop along on my stomach,
like a harbor seal on its haul-out, brushing aside cur-
tains of thick spiderwebs as I go. I was making that inelegant advance one afternoon in the dying days of winter,
begrudging the dirt and discomfort, certain I was called to
higher things in life than this, when I became immersed
in an indescribably lovely fragrance. In imagination I was
wafted away to a sunlit place brilliant with blossoms and
singing birds. The marvelous scent, it turned out, was
from a sarcococca growing in a sheltered nook by our
front door. Following mysterious pathways, the fragrance
had drifted down to the lowest available place and pooled
there under the house, creating a blissful sanctum that
could be reached only by crawling forward like an extreme
pilgrim, facedown in the dirt.

This admittedly under-the-bottom example typifies the
genius of the winter garden, which exists to create inspi-
ration at a time of bleakness. Were it to occur later in the
season, the sarcococca's fragrance, though still marvelous,
would be far less conspicuous amid the olfactory overload
from honeysuckles, roses, lilies, jasmine, and all the rest.

But blooming as it does, even before the hyacinths, it is a solitary superstar. Of such virtuoso turns is the winter garden made. The yeasty musk of English ivy mere weeks before Christmas is another such. So are the sinuous, bare twigs of Harry Lauder's walking stick dangling jaunty yellow catkins in February.

There is, no doubt, an inherent perversity in the matter of winter gardens, insofar as regions experiencing mild winters offer the best opportunities for them. The horticultural equivalent of the rich getting richer. But not without a price. It can be argued that there's a certain sanity to abandoning the garden for a season, to devoting oneself to other pursuits for a while. The all-season gardener runs the greater risk of obsession, of becoming, as in Winston Churchill's pithy definition of a fanatic, someone "who can't change his mind and won't change the subject." The hardy gardeners of Saskatoon and Denver may, thanks to their enforced period of horticultural hibernation, enjoy a mental equilibrium more elusive to coastal growers, who continue wallowing in the mud in mid-January. The southern California coast bears frightening testimony to the psychic hazards that await those who know no winter dormancy.

Still, if wallow we can, wallow we will, and British Columbia's south coast region perhaps enjoys the best of both worlds—sufficient wintry weather to toughen the spirit, but not so much as to render gardening entirely impractical. The coastal grower's winter garden tiptoes along the high ledge of the barely possible. The *Helleborus foetidus* may cringe through the worst of the weather, then swell handsomely after a few warming weeks. The evergreen *Clematis armandii* may rival the sarcococca for sweetness of scent only to die back to the ground or be killed outright, as ours was, by a brutal combination of wet and cold. The Christmas rose—a gleaming star of hope in the gloom of January—may have its waxy white blooms crushed beneath a coating of freezing rain. But conquest of adversity is at the heart of the winter garden, perhaps best symbolized by winter aconites, those sturdy little sunbursts that bloom so cheerfully during a warm spell in January. They close up and hang on for dear life during subsequent storms and resume blooming once conditions improve. They represent, like the winter gardener herself, a remarkable combination of tenderness and rugged perseverance.

Arguably the greatest benefit to be derived from the foul-weather performers is that they compel an attentiveness to, and appreciation of, small beauties in an otherwise bleak prospect. Compared with the later luxuriance of rhododendrons or roses, the small, scented flowers on Pink Dawn viburnum and the spidery little blooms on the Chinese witch hazel are almost laughably insignificant. But appearing amid a brooding gloom, these miniature marvels shine like beacons. Living as we do in a culture bloated with acquisitiveness, we might do worse than to contemplate the minimalist treasures of the winter garden, to consider the possibilities of doing better with less.

The experience may even lead to an unexpected moment of transcendence, as it did for us on another occasion in the depths of winter. We awoke on solstice morning, rather late, to a clear blue sky and a landscape whitened by hoar frost. Two nights before, a fierce winter storm had lashed us with wind and rain, knocking down power lines and causing us to huddle festively around candles. But the shortest day of the year dawned with a shimmering brilliance. Our woodland clearing steamed with rising mist, and the gardens gleamed every bit as pleasingly as on the finest summer morning.

Treetops caught the spirit first. The topmost twigs of the paperbark maple glowed tawny and warm in the crisp air. The tree's bark, curled like ancient parchments, caught the light and held it inside translucent scrolls. Cherry-red fruits on a Red Jewel crab apple tree glistened with drops of moisture, the tiny apples clustered like a galaxy of shining ornaments. Nearby the tall skeletons of Joe Pye weed, left over from fall blooming, stood etched with delicate fretwork in sunlight. Equally fine, the twigs of Japanese maples traced intricate patterns against blue sky, and their slender trunks showed a pale but vivid green. The trunks of ornamental cherry trees shone with a coppery luster. Everything seemed for the moment more intensely itself. Thickets of red-twigged dogwoods had never looked more emphatically red, nor their yellow-twigged cousins more energetically yellow. A variegated holly bush, catching the full sun, glowed like heaped yellow coals. So did a golden boxwood, sheared to a globe that shimmered green and gold. Variegated Persian ivy spilling over a stump looked radiant too, its broad leaves splashed with graphic yellows and greens. Oak-leaf hydrangea leaves showed a rich burgundy, and portly bergenia leaves shone like polished bronze. A cryptomeria smoldered with dusky browns and reds, and drifts of Autumn Joy sedums, left for structural interest, formed rusty archipelagoes through the perennial beds. Elegant heavenly bamboos fitted genially into the jubilation of the morning, their massed, thin leaves impressionist blends of yellows, greens, and reds. Perched on ancient cedar stumps, native red huckleberry bushes billowed like cumulus clouds of tiny, gray-green twigs.

On a morning like that, even the commonplace became special: a photinia bush—overplanted to the edge of ennui in these parts—seemed distinctively fresh in the sunlight, its big, glossy, green leaves contrasting brilliantly with its bright-red twigs. A leather-leafed viburnum underwent similar transformation, a youthful sparkle enlivening its coarse old foliage. Small cascades of arabis and aubrietia spilled over frosty stone walls, and on a stone pathway a carpeting of woolly thyme lay whitened by frost, like a miniature snowy forest seen from above.

On the dirtiest days, even the best-planned all-season garden is hard-pressed to impress. The day after solstice, we were back to a leaden sky, bitter wind, and filthy drizzle. But on a perfect winter morning, as that solstice was, the garden is a thing of heartening beauty and a hopeful omen for the days to come.

Hopeful omens are a prized commodity; I find that with age I'm increasingly oppressed by the gloom of winter. I dwell, perhaps unduly, upon the violence, injustice, and greed that plague the planet. On dark days the destruction of ecosystems seems irreparable, the poverty of millions insoluble. I might lose heart entirely if I weren't blessed to live in a corner of the continent where winter begins to loosen its grip early in the year.

No season suits the gardening temperament so well as spring. We gardeners are, at our pith, creatures of spring. The giddy green explosion of growth is our métier. The swelling and breaking of buds, the unfurling of crimped leaves—here is where the pulse begins to quicken, the lifeblood to rise persistent as sap. The earthsurge trembling all around us—manifest in exotic spathes of swamp lanterns, the primeval flowering stalks of petasites, the jubilant nubs of crocus and snowdrops emerging from frosty ground—is a stirring of ancient forces that hurl us into feverish action. Germination trays are sanitized, potting soil prepared, a preposterous number of seeds planted, cold frames rehabilitated, the greenhouse straightened up, beds of gloriously warming earth turned. (Oh, the ridiculous rapture of wriggling pink earthworms!) More tasks are undertaken and accomplished in an afternoon than would just a little while before have seemed possible in a week. Lengthening days of labor fall short of exhausting our enthusiasm. We are on fire, inspired in a way no other part of the year can approximate. Creaky limbs acquire the sinuous flexibility of a gymnast's as we caper about in the rock garden. Perched atop the orchard ladder, pruning shears in hand, we're bathed in pale sunshine, awash in an awareness of how fine a thing it is to be alive.

Spring is a season of sounds as much as sights, as a marvelous symphony begins to play. Winter's soundscape has been a monotony of wind and rain occasionally punctuated by a cryptic call from a raven in the woods or the screeching of bald eagles perched on an ancient snag. The sound of spring, at least its opening movement, is far more subtle. I was planting potatoes one chilly afternoon—narcissus, forsythia, and the early cherries were flowering—when I gradually became aware of an intense electric humming in the air. I couldn't detect where the sound was coming from, until I looked to the crown of a bigleaf maple that towers behind the vegetable garden. Though its lower limbs were still bare, the tree's topmost branches had broken into blossom, dangling tassels of small, greenish-yellow flowers. Hundreds of big bumblebees were buzzing from flower to flower in a feeding frenzy. The whole yard seemed to hum with excitement. I laid my spade aside and put my cranial tape on pause. I listened. Interwoven through the drone of bees were twitterings and chirps, whistles and cheeps coming from every direction. Rustlings in nearby bushes. The businesslike drumming of courting woodpeckers in the forest. Tentative croaks from amorous tree frogs. Beethoven couldn't have done it better.

Our garden is, most vocally in spring, a place of birds. Throughout the night the woods echo with the calls of owls. Cool mornings dawn in a chorus of birdsong. Rufous hummingbirds buzz through the sunlit garden, sipping nectar from the blossoms of peach trees and red flowering currant bushes. Clans of violet-green swallows swoop and glide, noisily negotiating who gets to nest in which box. Grumpy-sounding towhees rummage among fallen leaves in the shrubbery. The hoarse call of western tanagers is less exotic than their brilliant red, yellow, and black plumage. The plaintive notes of robins sing the evening down. "I value my garden more for being full of blackbirds than of cherries," Joseph Addison wrote. I don't know if I'd go quite that far, particularly during the protracted campaign waged each summer to prevent avian theft of our strawberries, raspberries, and blueberries, but we wholeheartedly welcome the returning birds as minstrels of spring, whistlers and singers as joyful as sunshine.

In the extended spring of the Pacific Northwest, sunshine is a very on-again, off-again arrangement. Spells of fine weather alternate with gray days of drizzle and wind. When it's too wet or cold to garden but there is no wind blowing, Sandy and I seize the opportunity for a bonfire in the forest. Winter storms have littered the forest floor with branches and have usually toppled several big trees. Other trees have died; our western hemlocks, though not yet oldsters, have been dying at a dismaying rate, apparently victims of climate change. Where it's safe to do so, we leave them standing as wildlife trees. Where not, I fell them and buck them up for firewood. Always there are branches by the truckload to be burned.

Years ago, Sandy and I abandoned burning, for the sake of a healthier atmosphere. Instead, we dragged the branches to selected spots where we stacked them in brush piles that would serve as wildlife habitat until they eventually decomposed back into the earth. However, complications arose. The volume of branches and logs leaped exponentially after a clear-cut behind our property exposed our trees to winter winds. Dozens of trees toppled. A sequence of exceptionally dry summers regularly pushed the forest fire hazard rating up to extreme. Historically, these coastal Douglas-fir woodlands experienced periodic ground fires that burned off debris on the forest floor while leaving mature trees undamaged. Now, by suppressing natural wildfires and allowing ground fuel to accumulate, Sandy and I had set the stage for what could quickly become a catastrophic forest fire. All of this was sufficient to overcome our reluctance to burn. Still, our course is one of moderation: larger logs and limbs are left to decompose where they've fallen; more flammable branches and tops are dragged to the pyre.

A bonfire started from scratch has a dynamic of its own, from the struck match, the crackle of paper and kindling, the catching of dry twigs, the piling on of ever larger branches to the eager roaring that confirms it's now a fire voracious to be fed. We often work for four or five hours straight, methodically hauling branches from a widening circle. It's exhilarating work, charged with a clarity of purpose. By evening, when the fire's a mound of glowing embers, we sit and take our ease, gratified by how large a patch of forest has been cleared of debris. It's no great mystery why cleansing fire rituals were important in so many ancient cultures, for there's an unmistakable psychic dimension to springtime burning: the elimination of what's dead or diseased, clearing out clutter, beginning afresh.

Burning times stir up old questions about the relationship of forest and garden, of the natural and the contrived environment. We've designed our place so that the two flow in and out of one another, and certainly the gardens are enhanced by being set among magnificent trees. But how deep into the forest should the work of the garden go? I don't mean planting exotic species in the woods, but clearing and tending, eliminating trees, limbing others up to open a viewscape, manipulating with ax and chain saw for our aesthetic pleasure. The trunks of craggy veteran firs and silver-gray cedars show to far finer effect without an untidiness of dead saplings and branches at their feet. But would the salamanders and varied thrush prefer a labyrinth of twigs and sticks for their own purposes? We are creators in the garden, inveterate manipulators, but in the forest we are caretakers at best, tenants whose tenure will soon pass. The forest will long outlast the garden and, with luck, reclaim it in the end.

Spring, however, does not encourage extended deliberation. It's a time of energy and activity, of enthusiastic undertaking. A bracing optimism illuminates every plan of action. The rambling rose that last summer posed such a menace to good order is now tidily confined to a newly built arbor. The pruning of roses alone—we have maybe sixty or seventy, mostly antique varieties—might be a daunting chore at a less-charged time of year. Not now. With secateurs and saw and loppers, I go after the thorny brutes, and they go after me. It is a fierce clash of wills. Blood is spilled, oaths are hurled, but the job gets done, and we're off to the next adventure.

So unbounded is my optimism that I take to uprooting dandelions with a firm conviction that this will be the last of them for the year. I pull them from the lawn by the hundreds; then we wash the roots and dry them for tea. Notwithstanding their health-giving properties, I persist in seeing them as a weed whose expansive tendencies ought to be curtailed. The intelligent part of myself knows that the dandelions will eventually defeat me, but for now all things are possible.

Spring reawakens a faith in the future, and nowhere is this more evident than in the vegetable garden. Rhubarb shoots and horseradish are already showing; the garlic, planted last fall, is growing splendidly. French sorrel, chives, corn salad, and chervil have overwintered nicely and will be ready for picking soon. The broad beans are up and running long before the last frost. We await the first spears of asparagus. Beds are dug, fertilized, and planted with early potatoes, peas, spinach, and arugula. Touching earth that is young again, we shed our wrinkled skins of cynicism. The springtime gardener is infused with the jubilant notion that what lies ahead is more promising than what has ever gone before.

This seasonal rejuvenation and the spiritual balance it imparts make it very difficult to leave the gardening life. I've spoken to many people compelled by age or infirmity to abandon gardening, but never yet, for all its work and worry, has anyone told me they were happy to let it go. Every once in a while Sandy and I discuss the merits of a year away from the gardens. Imagine all that time freed up to read books and listen to music, the blessed freedom to go travel the world. So what if things got a bit out of control, neglected-looking for a while? We could whip the place back into shape within a month or two the following year. So we tell ourselves. And yet, somehow, we've never quite managed this grand laying-down of rake and spade in favor of other pursuits. The rituals of renewal, when hands are plunged into the awakening earth, remain too compelling.

The commotion of growth rises as all the early stars come out—vivid falls of arabis and aubrietia; hosta leaves tinted with watercolor greens, blues, and yellows; clusters of common foxgloves raising medieval spires of white and mauve bells; the festive red flags of oriental poppies and stately pink towers of foxtail lilies. By the time the irises and peonies and delphiniums are rising to crescendo, the floodgates of sensuousness are wide-open. It is the point when, as Matthew Arnold put it, "the high midsummer pomps come on." Pausing to gaze into the blooms of clustered roses—a moss rose here, a Bourbon over there, a brilliant centifolia or sweetly perfumed damask—we are intoxicated in the purest sense of the term. The flaming silken petals of opium poppies run riot across the hillside as though on a Monet canvas. Ornamental alliums explode into astral galaxies of bloom. Clematis vines pour cascades of mauve and blue and white down their obelisks.

For a few incomparable weeks, all of nature seems to conspire in this midsummer dream. The longest days of the year open with morning sunlight radiant through the woodlands and end with warm, richly scented hours of gilded light. Veils of fragrance from the lilies mingle with the heady scent of honeysuckle, the spicy musk of dianthus, the citrus perfume of mock oranges. The first fawns of the year tiptoe out of the woods, impossibly lovable despite the damage they'll wreak later on. Swallows fledge in a burst of aerial acrobatics. Swallowtail butterflies drift like floating petals, alighting on the flowers of dame's rocket to sip sweet nectar as the gods and goddesses of old were said to do.

The sense of urgency that drove us through the spring is gone. Awash in beauty, we are giddy and pensive and teary by turns, subsumed in a lovely wholeness. Summer's the season when the reasoning left brain slinks away to the shade and the Dionysian side of ourselves emerges. Calculation lies abandoned; plots and schemes and purposeful determinations are forgotten. The regrets and disappointments of the past evaporate; anxieties about what is to come shrink to nothing. We're remembering lines from old lyric poems, the faces of former lovers, fragments of fantastic apparitions. We are lifted outside ourselves. Hours can pass unnoticed as we wander the gardens. Everything is the present. We are at the apex of an arc, a point of perfect balance. We know in our bones that we will not do better than this. Ever. To be in a place of beauty, at peace with those we love, content with the course of our lives— is this not the real object of our craving? So simple a thing, and yet so elusive. Why do we humans insist upon resisting the perfection of the present? Why give credence to cynics who dismiss such experiences as idleness or sentimentality? All of spirituality, all of art, strives to attain it. And here it is, devoid of striving, beyond desire.

But, like midsummer itself, we can linger only so long in this exalted state. We must return to earth, or who knows what might become of us. Soon enough, too soon, our busy other half has reasserted itself, scuttling out to get the strawberries picked and jam made and, yes, you do have a dentist's appointment tomorrow, not to mention that important meeting at work. But our midsummer dream still enlightens the "real" world through which we move. As this astonishing metamorphosis repeats itself year after year, I increasingly suspect that the magic one is the real world and the fussy "reality" the figment.

Late summer's given over to harvesting the fruits of previous labor. Earlier strawberries, raspberries, and rhubarb are followed now by blackberries, bayberries, and blueberries, figs, grapes, peaches, plums, and pears. Baskets of plump, vine-ripened tomatoes, buckets of beans and beets, an exorbitance of zucchinis—there seems no end of produce to be picked and processed. All with the gratifying sense of "putting things down" for the winter, in outright defiance of transnational food conglomerates.

Summer slowly wearies its way toward fall. Though at dawn the lawns are drenched with dew, it will not rain for weeks. As the days shorten, the earth begins to shrivel.

The woods are brittle with drought. Red-legged frogs hop dispiritedly among scorched mosses. The lawns are a mangy yellow, panting in the sun. The garden grows tired. It is stitched together with silvery spiderwebs. Hydrangeas, Japanese anemones, and late summer phlox do their best to maintain a bold show, eventually bolstered by Autumn Joy sedums. Tussock grasses glow with bronze and red tints. But everything awaits the rain. Grasshoppers and crickets fiddle scratchy laments. Tree frogs high in the canopy call to the sky for moisture.

Finally their incantations are answered. Dark clouds gather over the mountains to the west. There is a cooling restlessness in the air, an expectant tension in which every living thing holds its breath. Then a scattering of drops. A pause. The silence is absolute. A chill breeze shakes the dusty leaves awake. At last a heavy rain begins to fall. Each droplet seems enormous, splattering against parched surfaces, splashing off months of dust. There's a joyful dripping and trickling and dribbling from every leaf and stalk. Sucking up moisture, the earth exhales, breathes freely, letting its stiffened limbs relax.

After the first few rains have done their restorative work, the woods and gardens come back to life. A fresh flush of grass revitalizes parched lawns. Colchicums burst into flower, as welcome as their springtime cousins, the crocuses. Carpet mosses on the forest floor return from what looked like death by desiccation, clothed in a brilliant new green. Some of the roses are inspired to a repeat blooming. This is the second coming of the garden, shorter and less abundant than the first, but illumined by the golden tones of the low-slung sun and the frost-sharpened colors of fall. Soon the Japanese maples and liquidambars, the Korean dogwoods and Persian parrotias, the oaks, cherries, beech and smoke trees ignite the landscape with fiery reds, oranges, and yellows. The ginkgo trees turn a pale and perfect yellow, then cast off their leaves in a sudden, dramatic disrobing. The bigleaf maples follow suit, though at a more leisurely pace. Their large, dry leaves rustling down create one of autumn's best-remembered sounds. Birds return to the garden en masse; flocks of chickadees come swirling in to feed on the berries of pyracantha and crab apples. Robins and pileated woodpeckers pluck the red fruits of dogwoods. Western flickers strip the blue elderberries of their fruit.

The gardener is as busy as the birds, bustling about with the renewed energies of autumn. Now's the final episode of gathering and storing: harvesting apples, bringing in the winter squash, picking buckets of chanterelle mushrooms in the forest, and stacking the winter's firewood. Raking leaves for leaf mold and making compost from the garden's detritus. Putting away the garden fixtures, battening things down, and preparing for the dark times ahead.

The welcome rains of September become the howling gales of November. Deciduous trees are stripped of their last leaves. The webs of garden spiders hang in tatters. The autumn birds are long since fled. Dry through the summer, our little creek flows again beside the house. The garden is a wreckage of its former self. "The last hollyhock's fallen tower is dust," writes the poet Laurence Binyon. "The reddest rose is a ghost." Facing the onset of winter, we indulge ourselves with the customary autumn meditations on death and dying and the transitoriness of life itself. "My very heart faints and my whole soul grieves / At the moist rich smell of the rotting leaves," mourned Tennyson.

It's a poignant scene, no question about it, but no more permanent than any of its predecessors. It too will pass, is already passing. And if it does not pass, if our circle is at last truly broken, we join defiantly with Michel de Montaigne, who wrote: "I want Death to find me planting my cabbages, worrying neither about it nor the unfinished gardening."

Chaos Theory in the Garden

ONE COMES OCCASIONALLY upon closet gardeners, clandestine gardeners, perhaps even guerrilla
gardeners, individuals who keep their predilec-
tion for horticulture discreetly out of sight. Their gardens
remain strategically removed from public view, and they
themselves are all but silent on the topic. Confronted by
such an enigma, the inquiring mind would naturally ask:
why this dissimulation? Why this disinclination to openly
reveal one's involvement in the fluid and fecund world of
the garden?

The answer, I believe, can be found in something I
call, rather grandly, Chaos Theory in the Garden. The
theory posits that the behavior of gardeners, while ostensibly devoted to the creation of the beautiful and the good,
in reality manifests a pattern of mental and emotional

disequilibrium that some find a source of embarrassment. Henry James described how "the slowly but surely working poison of the garden-mania begins to stir." Lewis Gannit wrote, "Gardening is a kind of disease. It infects you, you cannot escape it." A poisonous mania and a disease both—these are the hard realities of the gardening life that Chaos Theory attempts to address. While horticultural therapists and others of their ilk trumpet the garden as a place of calm and healing, a sanctuary in which the strife and turmoil of the outer world are left behind, Chaos Theory posits the opposite: that the pandemonium afoot in a garden makes the rest of life seem positively bland and predictable.

It's commonly understood among gardeners that, no matter how long we've been at it, an infinitude of insights yet awaits us. Some of us choose to learn not through tranquil study and instruction but rather in the killing fields of trial and error. At one point in my education as a gardener, for instance, no longer willing to tolerate pots of anemic springtime seedlings leaning toward the light from every window ledge in the house, I installed in our unheated greenhouse a proper germination chamber, with a heat coil beneath and grow lights suspended above. This represented a quantum leap in our germination technology, one that promised spectacular sproutings of vegetation.

Noticing at the local nurseries what I considered an unconscionable rise in the price of potting soil (an earlier slip on the learning curve had cured me of the urge to make my own), I purchased an enormous sack of perlite, thinking I might cut my losses on the soil by cutting it with perlite. The initial response from my seeds was encouraging: onions, squash and tomatoes, aubergines and peppers sprouted brilliantly in their warm and well-lit trays. I watered them diligently from a big garbage can full of sun-warmed stinging-nettle tea, imagining undreamed-of vegetative vigor.

Soon came the first intimations of trouble—a lack of vivacity in the seedlings, an apparent slackening of resolve. I concluded for no good reason that they were getting too chilled at night, and I started draping a sheet of clear plastic over the lights, thereby forming a tentlike chamber. Within days it became apparent that I was flirting with disaster. Squash leaves crumpled like used paper napkins, aubergines turned a shade of purple more appropriate to their fruit than to their leaves, and the peppers had no pep at all. In the time-honored tradition of the underinformed gardener, I vacillated between believing I was watering too liberally—a diagnosis leading to periods of drought that would desiccate a cactus—and a conviction that I was watering too sparingly, resulting in periodic drenchings sufficient to drown a bog rosemary.

Slow and painful deaths ensued.

What had happened, I concluded at the postmortem, was that my pots of perlite-soil mix had, when combined with nettle tea and enclosed in the warm chamber, slowly baked to the consistency of Rice Krispie squares. The roots of my seedlings had, like the fellow in the TV ad about erectile difficulties, been unable to penetrate. One helpful associate chimed in at this point to the effect that you can develop malignant tumors from eating vegetables grown in perlite. Score one for Chaos Theory.

Humiliated, I sped to a nursery and purchased several flats of robust-looking replacement plants. By now, things were considerably behind schedule, and haste was of the essence. I set to planting out the replacements, working a handful or two of fertilizer—blended canola meal, bone-meal, kelp meal, and lime—under each plant. When digging over the vegetable beds in spring, I now and then broadcast a tiny sprinkling of boron to correct an alleged boron deficiency in our soil. On this occasion, pressed for time as I set to plant out my broccoli and cauliflowers, then later squashes, aubergines, peppers, and tomatoes, I took the kind of shortcut much favored by Chaos Theory gardeners: instead of broadcasting the boron beforehand, I included it in my fertilizer mix. I won't belabor the ugly scenes that ensued: stunted and horrid contortions in the brassicas, grotesque writhings and sickening chlorosis in the tomatoes, and, eventually, mercifully, death among the transplants.

As any defensive gardener might, I cast about for cul-prits, but the usual suspects—slugs, sow bugs, cutworms, root maggots—were nowhere in evidence. I fell back on the gardener's most reliable standby: blaming the weather. I offered some particularly damning public commentary on global climate change and the perfidy of the petroleum industry. At last, reluctantly, I examined the case objectively. I did a bit of research, which is something the Chaos Theory gardener on principle avoids. I learned that plants will suffer deficiencies if planted in soil containing less than one part per million of boron, but will suffer even more from an excess of boron—meaning anything more than three parts per million. How any citizen of the realm slouching around in gum boots and coveralls is expected to calculate the difference between one and three parts per million in their soil is the kind of absurdity Chaos Theory gardeners know to be all too commonplace. But, irrefutably, I'd given my transplants a toxic dose of boron through my slapdash application. Moron with the boron!

Chaos Theory is not limited to individual initiatives. Collective undertakings have a robust magnifier effect in the advance of Chaos, and perhaps none plays so pivotal a role as the compulsive attending of flower and garden shows. No sooner are the Christmas decorations down than the early shows begin, with people fighting their way through ice storms to dreary convention centers riotous with forced blooming bulbs. Spring and early summer are clogged with consecutive shows, so that dashing from one to the next becomes a full-time occupation.

Outdoor shows generally require a heavy, pelting rain to be considered truly successful. Display gardens are battered down; merchandise in the booths is soaked; people selling ice cream and cold lemonade stand like shivering ghosts at their deserted stalls. Triflers stay away in droves, but crackpot gardeners are entirely undeterred. "Well, we needed the rain, didn't we?" they say jauntily while the monsoon buckets down around them. As with earthquakes and tornadoes, legends are born at these storm-tossed events: many survivors still remember Vancouver's VanDusen Flower and Garden Show of '97, when it rained so relentlessly the Great Lawn turned into a quaking bog into which several innocent passersby were sucked, as into quicksand, never to be seen again. Conversely, indoor shows frequently take place during the nicest weather of the year, when reasonable people would be home gardening, not gawking at the latest trends in gazebo construction. I vividly remember attending one indoor show held in an airtight hockey arena that trapped the body heat of several thousand crazed showgoers and turned the place into a floriferous sauna. People wandered around, sweating profusely and clutching newly purchased compost forks, as though in a cartoon version of hell. One particular show—which only fear of a defamation suit prevents me from naming—is notorious for packing people in like celery seedlings. Successful participants simply wedge themselves into the slow-moving mudslide of humanity and are carried along, able to see nothing but the back of the person immediately ahead. At the end of the day they're disgorged onto the sidewalk with little idea of what was in the show. (This at least saves one from toxic overexposure to shrieking banks of forced tulips.)

The big shows are usually built around display gardens, which can range from the sublime to the subliminal. Oftentimes there's a show theme to inspire the garden designers—Down the Garden Path, A Walk through Time, The Sensuous Garden, et cetera. But, as delightful and whimsical as the display gardens may be, most people would still rather go shopping. And, truth to tell, the show marketplace is where the real action takes place. You have to admire the salespeople. They are a breed apart, street-smart pitchmen and -women of astounding endurance and loquacity. Poets and philosophers both, they mesmerize the passing crowds with anecdotes about the miraculous powers of polyunsaturated water or the unarguable superiority of double-density downspouts. At virtually every show an Olympic champion of touts emerges, a character of such captivating eloquence, such marvelous discernment as to what will inflame the shopper's imagination, that everyone in the place is wandering around happily clutching a new magic all-purpose whatchamacallit.

The newest "must have" sensation is never, ever, a fool-proof garden sprayer, though. I've arrived at the conclusion that there's no such thing and never will be. Chaos Theory is seldom more graphically in evidence than during those bracing days of midwinter when it's time to give the fruit trees their annual three applications of dormant oil and lime sulfur. This ritual is ostensibly intended to control the hordes of mites, hoppers, scales, thrips, blisters, curls, and other nuisances that assail our fruit trees and bushes. In reality, its chief function is to drive the gardener into a state of purple-faced rage at the inventors, designers, manufacturers, distributors, and retailers of whatever sprayer you've been cursed to own. Why is it, you ask yourself, that human ingenuity, for all its triumphs—space probes, super-computers, microsurgery—cannot devise a garden sprayer that you or I can successfully employ for our modest spraying needs? We don't ask much, just simple competence.

You know the routine as well as I do. You mix your dormant oil and lime sulfur. You're never absolutely certain that you've got your milliliters-to-liters ratio right, metric mysteries lacking as they do the accessibility of, say, half a pint to the gallon. Nevertheless, you get the mixture, such as it is, into the sprayer and set off to give the fruit trees their due. Aware of the hazards of possibly toxic substances, you dress for the occasion—a battered hat, goggles to protect the eyes, and a bandanna covering nose, mouth, and lower face. A rubber jacket and double trousers—in my case, the outer being a pair of black polyester dress pants that have repeatedly proved themselves impervious to penetration by moisture or air. Gum boots and thick rubber gloves like oyster shuckers wear. You offer up incantations that no distinguished visitors will appear while you're wobbling about in this ludicrous getup.

Having outlasted several generations of unsatisfactory sprayers, I'm currently stuck with a model, by a well-known manufacturer, that boasts a cylindrical polyethylene compression tank with a maximum capacity of just under two gallons. The pump assembly is inserted into its top. A short rubber hose connects to a handle with a control valve, which in turn connects to a metal extension from which the spray will theoretically spew. To pressurize the tank before spraying, it's necessary to release the pump handle, lift it all the way up, and vigorously plunge it down into the pump cylinder, repeating the pump stroke until the desired pressure has built within the tank.

Fifty pumps later, you're pouring sweat inside your rubber and polyester swaddling clothes. Your goggles are fogged up, and you can't breathe through the confounded bandanna. Nor has any substantial pressure been built. This may be because you've neglected to tighten the control valve, or perhaps because the plunger cap has atrophied during months in storage. Or maybe because the cylinder gasket is leaking. You trudge back to the shed, make the necessary corrections, and retrace your steps to the orchard. Pump, pump, pump, and this time—ah! the pressure's building beautifully. Aiming the extension nozzle at an apple tree, you squeeze the control valve. Voila! A quick squirt of liquid. Then nothing. You remove the nozzle cap and clean out the clogged discharge hole. You try again. A fitful spit and nothing more. At this point you recollect that you neglected to thoroughly clean out the tank and hose after using it for a final time last year. Old goop must be plugging the apertures. Back you go to the shed to clean the unit.

Preoccupied as you are with composing sufficiently vile curses to demean the sprayer, you forget to release the pressure in the tank before unscrewing the hose connection. The resulting blast of pressure just about blows your head off. The tank topples over, spilling most of your precious spray mixture on the ground. After a matching blast of florid vulgarisms, you flush out and clean the nozzle body and cap orifice, then the control valve, the supply tube, and extension tube. All of the unit's assembly connection points contain a tiny rubber O-ring or V-ring, at least one of which you will lose during the flushing process.

Back to the orchard. Another fifty pumps. Pressure like you wouldn't believe. You aim the nozzle, squeeze the control valve, and out flies a marvelous jet of liquid. You adjust the nozzle cap to produce a finer spray, but this causes the jet to stop completely. Recognizing you can't achieve the fine tuning required while wearing rubber gloves, you discard the cumbersome gloves, just as you've long ago discarded the steamed-up goggles and gagging bandanna. After repeated adjustments of the squirting nozzle cap, your hands are drenched in liquids you highly suspect of being carcinogenic. Every time you squeeze the control valve, you get another squirt of the stuff up your arm (likely because of the missing O-ring). Profanity by this point has achieved epic eloquence.

The remainder of the expedition is spent floundering around the orchard, pumping and adjusting valves and nozzles in a vain attempt to get the desired misty spray. You settle for a limp dribble, which you sprinkle on the trees by shaking the extension at them, like a priest shaking his aspergillum to dispense holy water. Invariably a brisk wind kicks up at this point and blows the dribbling liquid back onto your face and sodden clothes. The wind, you realize, is a precursor to sudden showers, which will wash off whatever oil and lime sulfur has gotten onto the trees before it can achieve its intended purpose.

In the end, exasperated by the whole wretched business, you dump the remaining mixture onto the strawberry beds, telling yourself at least it'll keep gray mold at bay next summer, and then pitch the bloody sprayer into the shed. You know you should drain and clean the apparatus before storing it away again. And you will; maybe tomorrow. Meanwhile, you stomp indoors and vent to anyone who'll listen about the infuriating incompetence of the persons who design and manufacture garden sprayers.

Beset on all sides by such inadequacy, and with Chaos Theory continuing its inexorable march forward, harried gardeners begin to lose their grip. They take to asking themselves increasingly bizarre questions, such as: Is there a risk of contracting mad cow disease through handling bonemeal? Laugh if you want, but the question has a certain compelling logic. Untold thousands of potentially mad cows have been slaughtered in recent years, their bones rendered down and retailed to innocent gardeners at more per pound than sirloin steak. What substantive proof do any of us have that the bonemeal we buy did *not* in fact originate in a mad cow?

I dislike this sort of speculation, because it makes one think about things. That's seldom a good idea. Bonemeal is such a gratifyingly granular substance, as soft as white sand on a tropical beach, as benignly organic as camomile tea. But perhaps it's only the "meal" bit in the name that soothes our sensibilities, reminding us of sleepy Sunday dinners with the family. If they called it "ground bones," would we be as complacent? Or would we shrink in revulsion from intimations of mortality, of skeletons and grave robbers and Dickensian scoundrels whispering in the fetid corners of foul boneyards? When I'm sprinkling a cup of bonemeal under the tulip bulbs, I'd rather consider its great calcium content, how it almost glows with the phosphorus so essential for good root formation and vigorous new growth.

Once upon a time we used blood meal in the garden, too, until I made the mistake of thinking about that. Whose blood exactly are we dealing with here? I asked myself. How spilled and how caught? All I wanted was a little organic nitrogen, thank you very much; instead, I found myself assailed by images of lowing beasts being driven into a blood-spattered abattoir. After such a vision, no amount of rationalizing could restore blood meal's former allure. I tried to convince myself it was preferable that the blood be put to good use rather than being flushed down a polluting gutter but to no avail. Just looking at poor love-lies-bleeding, *Amaranthus caudatus,* became a dreadful reminder of my complicity in bovine slaughter.

Same thing happened when I let myself think about peat moss. Gardening on the sievelike sand and gravel of our property, I'd come to love peat moss, its miraculous moisture retentiveness, the marvelous compactedness of its big, white plastic bales. I began, harmlessly enough, by thinking of my Celtic forebears gathered around a peat fire in a picturesque thatched cottage, singing Gaelic tunes while gnawing on potatoes. But once started, thinking's hard to stop, and pretty soon I'd hopped from Riverdance to contemplating the hapless bogs from which the moss is ripped, at what accelerated rate, to stuff those plastic bales in every nursery in Canada from here to Newfoundland and Labrador.

No, I strongly advise against too much thinking on these matters. It only accelerates the advance of Chaos Theory. My companion and I have never used feather meal, for example, but if we did I wouldn't dwell upon whose feathers were involved or how they were extracted or what became of the featherless birds. We do use kelp meal for adding potassium and trace elements, and there's a mighty temptation while applying it to picture hearty maritimers in gum boots and thick sweaters striding along windswept beaches to gather gleaming kelp amid the cries of gulls and the thunder of surf. But I resist this temptation, as I do temptations of the flesh or the devil, because one thought would lead ineluctably to another, and who knows what illicit goings-on might be found clinging like crabs to kelp?

Hollowed-out peat bogs, naked chickens, boron misapplications, dysfunctional sprayers—no good will come from dwelling on any of them. And on the bonemeal bit, you can find any number of stir-crazed gardeners who'll testify that you can handle it for years, fondle it if you want to, without any mental side effects at all. They are persons entirely embraced by Chaos, the guardian spirit of gardens, and it's not to be wondered at that the more discreet among them opt to keep their condition removed from public view.

Garden Clubbing

MUCH OF THE frenzied activity encountered within the gardening community has less to do with gardening than with the business of garden clubs. Plant sales, seed exchanges, lectures, garden tours, seminars, bus trips to distant pleasure grounds—garden clubs seethe in season with more energy than a nuclear reactor. And the molten core of this hurly-burly is invariably the garden club meeting. (Certain organizations go by the far grander name of "horticultural society," but their antics are indistinguishable from those of the homier "garden clubs," and for our purposes shall be considered identical.)

As soon as you draw within a few blocks of the club's monthly meeting place, you come upon crowds of people hurrying in the same direction. Many are bearing flats loaded with seedlings, or hanging baskets and urns bulging with plants, or plastic garbage bags stuffed with roots and tubers. By the time you squeeze into the parking lot, the hordes of plant-bearers resemble leaf-cutter ants dragging foliage back to their nest.

The meeting place is typically a cavernous hall, dimly lit and lacking in aesthetic appeal—the kind of gloomy precinct that spells failure to unfortunate wedding receptions or high school reunions. But not to garden clubs. With members still arriving in droves, there's already a babble of voices inside, hoots and cries of laughter, a commotion of comings and goings. Tables arrayed at the front door are staffed by cheery volunteers busy signing up new members, dispensing name tags and door-prize tickets, and hawking raffle tickets with the skill of Egyptian marketplace merchants.

Everywhere you look, people are milling around, laughing and smiling and carrying on as though there were free martinis on offer. Over in the kitchen, volunteers are laying out platters heaped with cakes and cookies and fighting with cantankerous coffee urns that are guaranteed to never have the coffee perked on time. The few tables in the hall not groaning under the weight of goodies are heaped with plants—for a competition, or for sale, or simply for display. Eccentric-looking bystanders scrutinize the plants as though they held the secret of life (which, of course, they do).

In the fullness of time, the club president calls the meeting to order. This is easier said than done, as most members are so busy talking they don't hear the summons. Garrulous babbling continues until the president is compelled to threaten the merrymakers with abuse. As the hubbub subsides, the president seizes control. Club presidents are a breed apart, generally commanding personalities with a pronounced streak of masochism. They are like union bosses in the glory days of Big Labor—street-smart strategists able to mold the smoldering resentments of the membership into a bold plan of action. Overachievers themselves, they hold club members to the same high standard of performance and are frequently dismayed by the frivolousness of the membership at large. Authoritative studies have consistently detected a correlation between garden club presidency and the overconsumption of antidepressants.

After the general membership has been welcomed, new members and guests are asked to show themselves, which is scarcely necessary since they are distinguished by expressions of complete bafflement. The novices are roundly cheered and respond with nervous smiles.

Many clubs then have the secretary read the minutes of the previous month's meeting. Broadly speaking, club secretaries are persons afflicted with extremely poor hearing, as a consequence of which their minutes bear little resemblance to reality. As well, many secretaries have trouble remembering people's names, so a considerable amount of time is spent identifying errors and omissions and amending who exactly said what, exactly, at the last meeting. The situation is complicated by the fact that most members' memories are just as fuzzy as the secretary's. Conflicting versions of what was said or decided are advanced, with the result that the amended and corrected minutes are no closer to reality. By the time the minutes are accepted, the secretary is so flustered she's incapable of accurately recording tonight's business arising from the minutes—even if she could hear it.

Mercifully, the president rescues the situation by marching the membership through the list of planned activities for the coming month. Since together these are enough to exhaust a finely trained decathlon athlete, a multitude of questions arise as to when and from where the coach will leave for a particular outing, and so on, all of which the president refers to the pertinent committee chair. A discussion ensues as to whether the committee chair should answer the questions now or defer them until she delivers her committee report. Opinions are divided. The meeting threatens to dissolve into rank anarchy, but the president reins things back in by ruling that all questions will be dealt with under individual committee reports. Residual grumbling fades gradually, like retreating thunder.

Next, the treasurer is called upon to give a report. Almost all treasurers are cursed with a shiftiness of appearance, and it's generally accepted that their accounts of receipts and expenditures are to be taken with a grain of salt. Jokes are bandied about concerning how many trips the treasurer's been taking to Las Vegas of late. Adeptly she deflects potential difficulties by explaining that any discrepancies in the cash flow can be attributed to the fact that heads of committees have, despite numerous pleas from the treasurer, once again been tardy in getting their receipts in. The heads of committees, when called upon to give an accounting, ignore the treasurer's insinuations and describe the work of their particular committee with such enthusiasm that rounds of applause break out. Certain heads of committee, in fact, are regularly suspected of plotting a coup d'état to oust the president and treasurer and to install themselves and their cronies in the power positions. It's widely understood that the secretary, being as nonpartisan as she is incompetent, will be allowed to continue in her current position.

Some clubs are blessed with a person of particular horticultural expertise who now gives a brief—or sometimes not so brief—presentation on a specific plant or problem, then fields questions from the floor. It's an unspoken rule of garden clubs that questions be asked in such a quiet voice and using such convoluted diction that nobody in the room, including the expert, has any idea what the question is about. Marvelously, this seldom detracts from the luminousness of the answer.

By this point we've arrived at the great dividing line among clubs. Some now introduce the guest speaker and compel the audience to sit through the lecture with stomachs rumbling and the aroma of perking coffee permeating the room. Other clubs have an intermission at this juncture. Everyone bolts for the cakes and cookies (though the coffee's still not ready) and the party's on! It's an abiding mystery how these revelers can gobble such an astonishing volume of date squares, shortbread cookies, Nanaimo bars, butter tarts, and lemon squares and still get to sleep that night any place other than on the ceiling.

Calling the carousers back to order proves a daunting task, even for as formidable a personality as the president, but eventually a semblance of order is restored. If he has not been fortunate enough to make his presentation before the intermission, the guest speaker will now be introduced. Before that can happen, the guest speaker's introducer is introduced. Invariably, the introducer begins by describing the guest speaker as someone "who needs no introduction." One might thereby conclude that the introductory remarks will be brief, but it is soon revealed that the lack of a need for introduction will in no way hamper the introducer from launching into a peroration of unimaginable length and complexity, during the course of which the guest speaker's accomplishments and attainments, both real and imaginary, are paraded for the admiration of all.

As the introductory remarks wear on, enlivened by anecdotes and personal reflections, the guest speaker, glancing furtively first at his watch and then at the audience, becomes aware of two facts. The first is that most of the time allotted for his speech—"You must be finished by nine o'clock!" he's been told beforehand in no uncertain terms—has been devoured by the introduction. His second realization is that a significant segment of the audience has by this point—notwithstanding stratospheric blood-sugar levels—fallen asleep. Most guest speakers are highly strung individuals given to emotional disturbances if things don't go precisely as planned. Stranded on the headlands of an interminable introduction, the speaker may be assailed by strange facial tics and twitches that will undercut much of what he has to say.

A critical decision previously arrived at by the guest speaker has involved whether or not to give an illustrated presentation. The advantages of not including visual imagery are considerable: because the room lights will not be dimmed, furtive snoozing by audience members is more difficult to get away with. Plus, the opportunity for technical foul-ups is reduced. True, there are still the sound system and the microphone to deal with. Most microphones, like most personal computers, are cunningly designed so that, partway through using them, something will go awry. Deafening shrieks and sonic booms erupt for no reason (which at least serves the purpose of jolting audience members awake). Thereafter, more often than not, the microphone will simply stop working. Undeterred, the guest speaker endeavors to bellow a cappella, a bravura performance compromised only by audience members calling, "Speak up!" "Can't hear you!" "Louder!"

The opportunities for disaster increase exponentially when visual aids are added to the mix. Some guest speakers favor trundling in a truckload of plant material, for each specimen providing a description of its botany, taxonomy, mythology, cultivation, and uses both historical and contemporary. These speakers tend to be recent graduates of institutes of higher learning offering degrees in horticulture and landscape design. More seasoned speakers—apprised of the average garden club's limited tolerance for historical and taxonomical minutiae—prefer the more populist approach of creating onstage from their massed plant specimens a floral display in a vase or planter or hanging basket. These attempts invariably end in debacle. The plants simply won't cooperate. The colors are all wrong; upright elements are too gawky, prostrate ones too flaccid. With no honorable way out, the hapless guest speaker plunges from one miscalculation to another, jamming in new plant material and tearing out old, scattering potting mix, savagely stripping unwanted leaves from stems, and finishing up with what everyone recognizes as a travesty. Hoping to carry the day by chutzpah, if not by finesse, the speaker proclaims: "Now there's something new and different! Isn't that more exciting than the same old same old, eh?" Whether from genuine enthusiasm or simple relief, the audience salutes the guest speaker and his varicose vase with thunderous applause.

An alternative is for the guest speaker to rely upon slides or a PowerPoint presentation, and here the chances of catastrophe are unlimited. Slide projectors are notoriously finicky, and rare indeed is the garden club whose membership includes anyone with a rudimentary comprehension of how a slide projector functions. Within minutes of starting, the projector refuses to advance the next slide, choosing to show the same one over and over. Or each image is blurrily out of focus. Is the autofocus on or off? Who knows? Or a real crowd-pleaser: a slide gets jammed inside the projector. No amount of prying, tipping, or shaking can dislodge it. Or the projector bulb burns out, and there's no replacement bulb on hand. As often as not, the cantankerous coffee urns blow a fuse in the kitchen and power dies throughout the building. The guest speaker is left twisting in the wind. The crowd grows restive.

This same effect can be more dramatically attained through the wonders of a PowerPoint presentation. Images are made to come and go, as though by magic. Enlargements and diminishments, illuminating graphics, headings, and subtexts interweave on-screen as sinuously as a snake through dried leaves. Until the gremlin that resides inside the guest speaker's laptop decides to act up. The screen goes suddenly blank. An insistent cursor appears from nowhere. Strange menus start popping up. The guest speaker abandons the podium and dashes to his laptop, tripping over microphone wires en route. Frantic tapping at the keyboard only makes matters worse. Bizarre images begin appearing on the screen. Gasps from the audience. What exactly does Pamela Anderson reclining in her underwear have to do with new strains of Hagley hybrids? Eventually the guest speaker staggers to a conclusion and is greeted with lackluster applause. The official thanker congratulates the speaker on a brilliant presentation, one she's sure everyone agrees will be "a very hard act to follow." No one knows if the thanker is being ironic or not.

What in fact does follow is the evening's denouement— the awarding of door prizes and raffle prizes, which are usually potted plants of questionable provenance. Sometimes the guest speaker, still rattled by the unauthorized appearance of the Anderson tapes, is pressed into service as ticket selector. Each winning number called out is greeted with silence. The number is called again. Audience members who have been frantically searching their pockets and purses for ticket stubs now discover that they've left their reading glasses at home and can't make out the numbers. Commotion ensues as tickets are shown around and reading glasses passed about. If too much time passes, it's assumed that the winner has left early and thereby forfeited the winnings; other tickets are drawn and the commotion is repeated. By a process of attrition, all the prizes are finally awarded to the same two or three people. Most of them are relatives of the treasurer. The ritual complete and the crowd disintegrating, the president thanks everyone involved and adjourns the meeting. Club members, inspired anew by the glories of the gardening life, disperse into the night.

In the Land of the
Long White Cloud

HE TRIP WAS definitely off. The grand plan had been for me to lead a small group tour of New Zealand gardens during the first two weeks of February. Although we'd begun organizing the tour only a few months earlier, my travel consultant, Julia, and I had been confident of its appeal. After all, the time of year was perfect—the planting of onion seeds is the only legitimate claim on a northern gardener's attention in that bleak month. It would be late summer in New Zealand, a time when gardens would be awash in blowsy glory. Plus, New Zealand was very much on the cutting edge of the international gardening scene, especially after a Kiwi show garden captured the coveted gold medal at the 2004 Chelsea Flower Show. The *Lord of the Rings* movie trilogy had recently exposed the brilliance of New Zealand land-scapes to millions of viewers. Yes, our timing was impec-cable. All the elements were in place for a bang-up tour. Anticipating a crush of eager customers, we set a maxi-mum limit of fifteen, so as not to compromise the small-group experience.

But by Christmas, a mere five weeks before depar-ture, hardly anyone had signed up. We had a stalwart core of five, but that was insufficient to even cover costs. No, the tour must be cancelled, deposits returned, regrets expressed. Then Julia had a bright idea. This is one of the characteristics of travel consultants; they are prone to have bright ideas that would seldom occur to ordinary mortals. Here is what it was: we would eliminate the lux-ury coach and driver/guide, thereby radically reducing our costs. Instead, we would rent a twelve-passenger van that Julia would drive while I served as navigator, backup driver, and bon vivant.

Absolutely not, I said. The proposal would outrage our clients, who'd been promised something far tonier. In the confusion of the moment I failed to remember that we weren't dealing with clients, but rather with gardeners, a group whose zeal to tour gardens will brook no hindrance. When the notion of our restructured tour was presented to them, they leaped at it as salmon leap at a waterfall. It would be like a family outing, they enthused, so liberating, and vastly superior to the lock-step rigors of large group tours. So, against all odds, our minimalist trip was defi-nitely on.

We assembled at Vancouver International Airport on a cold, wet morning, Julia and myself plus our five adventuresome ladies—a demographic destined to earn me innumerable comments from gentlemen observers about how I was keeping my "harem" in line. Meanwhile, whoever it was who first proclaimed that "getting there is half the fun" had plainly never flown from Vancouver to Auckland. The first leg was a quick flight to San Francisco, which was pleasant enough. Landing at the spacious new airport there, we boarded an automated little shuttle train to carry us from one terminal to another. At the first stop, a passenger standing by the sliding doors addressed us all loudly: "There's an abandoned package on the floor under the backseat. It looks like a box of wine bottles, but you never know. I'm going to alert security." With that, he bounded out of the carriage. The doors swooshed shut, the train glided forward, and the digital woman's voice on the speaker system blandly welcomed us aboard again. Was the guy a nut? A bomber? We were in America, after all. I stared at the menacing carton, certain that the explosives it contained would be detonated any second.

After a brief consultation with Julia—bomb scares being the sort of contingency travel consultants have a grip on—I resolved to take action. At the next stop, I hailed a security guard lounging about the platform. I outlined the situation to him. His day enlivened by a bit of excitement, the security man instantly got on his walkie-talkie and then ordered us all off the train. It was whisked away, empty. A fair bit of grumbling ensued among some of the inconvenienced passengers, and a few ugly looks were cast my way. I badly wanted the train to explode a safe distance down the track, just to show them. It didn't. As the guard explained, the car would be shunted to a secure area where a bomb disposal team would deal with the package. I asked him how frequently this happened. Oh, two or three times a week, he told me, which somewhat diminished the drama quotient.

After a mind-numbing thirteen hours in the sky we touched down in Auckland. My brain felt like a cauliflower head left too long in the sun. We were herded through a rigorous inspection process to ensure we weren't importing any organisms potentially hazardous to the agricultural sector. This is a precautionary approach any gardener can appreciate, although in New Zealand's case it's a wee bit after the fact, since innumerable introduced species, both floral and faunal, have been wreaking havoc on the countryside for years. Are an estimated seventy million Australian possums less a menace than one mad cow? My camping gear was inspected and my tent sent off for fumigating. Our luggage was sent through X-ray machines.

I emerged from this process and out into the main terminal with our little group. But when I reached for my fanny bag, I realized with a shock I didn't have it on. I'd taken it off for the X-ray machine and obviously failed to retrieve it. Panic attack time. The bag contained my passport, plane tickets, credit card, and cash—my whole life was in that fanny bag, and if I didn't get it back, right now, all was lost, everything a ruin. But my route back into the security area was blocked by an enormous and utterly humorless guard who told me there was "no way" I was going back in there. After a description of my predicament failed to budge him, I thought to explain how closely I'd worked with one of his colleagues in San Francisco over the bomb. But he had no time for me and instead launched into an aggressive exchange with another passenger. Eventually a smiling female security person emerged with my fanny bag. I could have fallen to my knees and kissed her feet. For the second time in less than a day, catastrophe had been narrowly averted. Only a fool would have dismissed the possibility that a third, perhaps fatal, hazard awaited.

With the vapors of jet lag still trailing behind us, we found ourselves in Eden Garden, created on the site of an old quarry on the slopes of the tallest of Auckland's more than forty extinct volcanoes. Begun in the 1960s by a group of volunteers and now operated by a nonprofit society, Eden's a testament to the power of zealous gardeners to transform landscapes that have been degraded by other human activities. Home to the largest and most varied collection of camellias in the country, the garden has year-round interest with its native trees—the unfamiliar kauri, totara, rimu, puka, and titoki—ferns and shrubs, along with subtropical vireya rhododendrons, bromeliads, palms, and conifers. During our late-summer visit, hydrangeas and gardenias were on show, along with fuchsias, hibiscus, brunfelsias, strelitzias, and proteas. The place felt like a jungle, alive with the cries of exotic birds in the treetops. Already the dreary damp of home seemed a very long way away.

We stood on a lookout point atop Mount Eden enjoying panoramic views of Auckland and its surrounding waters, where myriad sailboats skimmed. A warm wind was blowing. The sky was high, white cloud with scattered patches of blue. Occasional light showers blew down and dried away instantly. Perfect. Except that within twenty minutes I had a nasty sunburn. Here was the flip side of paradise— the wobbling ozone hole that regularly settles over New Zealand, sending the UV Index skyward even on completely cloudy days. With the index stuck at "extreme" day after day, I took to slathering on sunscreen and swathing myself more thoroughly than the strictest Muslim matron.

We visited city gardener Dale Harvey, a boundless optimist and monologuist who showed us how he trained house sparrows to eat the aphids on his broccoli plants by first feeding the birds, with yellow ribbons strung near the food, then moving the ribbons to the broccoli plants. He similarly attracted New Zealand fantails for devouring mosquitoes. "You'd be slaving to get one peony to bloom here," he told us, standing beneath an enormous, flowering purple jacaranda. Part of his co-owned "Quarter Acre Paradise" was a tumult of magnolias and trumpet vines and bright apricot and orange flowering ginger. But he also does repeated plantings of annuals—"You can do five or six plantings a year for all-year bloom," he told us. The house exterior was encircled with innumerable pansies, petunias, and impatiens and covered with thousands of tiny lights. These are illuminated during the Heroic Gardens Festival, an annual tour of Auckland's finest gay- and lesbian-owned gardens that has raised hundreds of thousands of dollars for HIV/AIDS care.

Not far away we visited Peter Brady, who has surrounded his California Spanish Mission–style art deco house with a fantastic garden of aeoniums, echeverias, succulent bromeliads, pitcher plants, palm trees, drooping fuchsias, tree ferns, and pittosporum hedges, all interwoven with tropical masks and statuary, Balinese and Maori sculptures, glass floats, lengths of rope, and arrangements of stones. "It's a different sort of garden," Peter admitted. Standing in his undershirt with a parrot on his shoulder, he looked like an exotic escapee from a Somerset Maugham story. "I've gone a bit tropo in recent years."

Waitakere City is an Auckland suburb dubbed the "enviro-city" for its progressive policies in eco-housing, stream reclamation, and recycling. On a wooded hillside we visited Westridge, whose co-owner Geoff Haughey, an architect by trade, showed us around. He told us the garden was "a rose-free zone," hinting at what we would eventually recognize as a profound bipartisanship concerning roses within the New Zealand gardening community. Several rose enthusiasts within our group bristled but said nothing. We were distracted by the singing of a tui, called the parson bird for its little white bib. Its lovely, liquid song was a sprightly intermezzo amid the scratchy din of courting cicadas. Standing beside banks of succulent bromeliads with a gorgeous, orange-flowered clivia blooming under palm trees and tree ferns, Geoff said they'd never had a ground frost in the thirty years he'd lived there, but he complained about "the unbelievably revolting spring" they'd just suffered through. This lament failed to excite much sympathy in us, particularly as two of our group garden in northern British Columbia's Peace River country, where folks know a thing or two about revolting springs.

It's one of the principal problems for the gardener abroad, this compulsion to compare and contrast the features of home with those encountered elsewhere. The range of plant material available to the New Zealand gardener, particularly in the semitropical north, renders comparison hopeless for visiting Canadians—as was quickly confirmed at the Auckland Regional Botanic Gardens, where we were shown around by curator-manager Jack Hobbs. A great plantsman and a character of boundless energy, Jack had visited our Denman Island garden with a New Zealand television crew some years back. During his visit I had proved myself every bit as adept at not remembering my plant names as he had at knowing them. On such occasions I take to describing myself not as a gardener who writes but as a writer who gardens, and therefore one for whom allowances must be made. (In assemblages of writers I reverse the roles.)

Though relatively new, the Auckland Botanic Gardens boast comprehensive collections of African plants and New Zealand native species, many of them threatened, and over two hundred types of salvias, as well as extensive collections of dahlias, magnolias, palms, cycads, and subtropical plants from around the world. There's a heavy emphasis on community outreach and education: over eight thousand kids go through the garden's environmental programs each year. The Rose Display Trial Gardens aim to identify roses that can be grown in the region without spraying. The gardens are also home to the annual and hugely successful Ellerslie Flower Show in November, which attracts some seventy thousand visitors.

Jack escorted us to nearby Ayrlies, an 11-acre country garden of ponds and cascades, bridges and gazebos, sweeping lawns and superb vistas. It's the masterpiece of Bev McConnell, an eminent figure in the New Zealand gardening community. Regrettably, she wasn't at home, and we were instead shown around by a delightful lady named Penny, who laughed joyfully at every turn. And who wouldn't? The place was knock-your-socks-off gorgeous. We finished up at a naturalistic swimming pool nestled beneath a rockery of aloes and palms through which a small stream plashed. The main house nearby was draped with a brilliant cascade of Scarlet O'Hara bougainvillea. By this point we weren't wrestling with anything as wholesome as envy; I, at least, had descended into a grotesquely covetous cupidity.

Southeast of Auckland are the Bombay Hills, to Kiwis a dividing line of sorts. In Auckland we'd been told there was gardening north of the Bombay Hills—the extravagances to which we'd been exposed—and then there was gardening "south of the Bombay Hills," another matter entirely. Already satiated, and with a certain sense of relief, we packed our little van and headed south.

It's useful on an extended garden tour like ours—we were to visit twenty-six gardens in total—to vary the steady diet of gardens with an occasional foray into another area of interest. Our next stop, the city of Rotorua, a tourist destination renowned for its thermal waters, provided several such diversions. One was a concert of Maori song and dance and a *hangi* dinner at a marae site (traditional Maori village). No element of our itinerary had caused me greater misgivings. Poorly done, attractions of this type can be excruciating, as several hotels in the area seemed determined to demonstrate, with plastic-grass-clad natives twirling spears and dancing in the cocktail lounge. Our evening, orchestrated entirely by Maori people, suffered no such indignity. The hangi dinner, for which all the food is cooked together buried in an earth oven of stones, was superb, though I do wish I'd placed myself to better advantage when it came time to greet the person beside me in the traditional *hongi* (pressing of noses).

Our second diversion, a sheep show at the Agrodome, tilted more perilously toward tacky tourism. A great fan of sheepdogs and sheepdog trials, I approached this event with high expectations. Nobody does sheep like New Zealand—there are some forty million of them grazing the countryside—and one might legitimately anticipate a superb sheep show. We arrived at a large parking lot that was jammed with tour buses, each disgorging hordes of passengers. Our stately little van placed us somewhat above the madding crowd but not for long. We were herded into a large, barnlike building in which we sat on hard benches facing a raised stage at the front. A gangly character in sleeveless T-shirt and jeans bounded onto the stage, greeted us enthusiastically, and launched into the dismaying: "Now, who's visiting from Australia?" Roars from the Aussies. "Who's from Japan?" Polite expostulations from the Japanese. Et cetera. When at last Canada was called, our little rump of ladies shrieked with an enthusiasm that on a per capita basis far exceeded anything the larger contingents had managed. I'm uncertain whether I felt a surge of patriotic pride or not.

The show involved a representative from each of the nineteen breeds of sheep raised in the country being brought on stage and described by the host, who came to increasingly resemble a tattooed, aging punk rocker doing a John Cleese imitation. With his thick accent, a crummy sound system, and terrible acoustics, we couldn't hear a lot of what he had to say, which may have been for the best. He did garner points for shearing an uncooperative sheep in fairly respectable time. At various junctures audience members were brought onstage to look sheepish. The grand finale involved half a dozen heading dogs barking furiously while running across the backs of the assembled sheep, finally standing on their charges' backs in a dramatic tableau. The crowd loved it. In its own bizarre way the show wasn't half bad, but as we filed out of the Agrodome the curmudgeonly part of me couldn't help thinking that we too had been herded and shorn.

It seemed decidedly time to get ourselves back to the gardens, and some true beauties lay in wait. The first was Gordon Collier's newish garden in Taupo. Gordon's an iconic figure in the New Zealand gardening scene, an internationally recognized plantsman and writer who owned a renowned show garden before semiretiring four years ago with his wife, Annette, to a smaller property. It's fun to meet a celebrated expert like Gordon, but it's disconcerting to recognize how increasingly close in age you're becoming to people you picture as venerable old gardeners. His is a collector's garden, various parts of it modeled on gardens he has visited over the years—the fountains at Granada, clusters of irises based on the blue and gold of Giverny, a patch of drought-tolerant stalwarts inspired by Beth Chatto in England. Native kanuka and corokia hedges divide the garden into separate rooms, and other rare or exotic natives are tucked in here and there. "This one's known as the Bushman's Friend," he told us, fingering a broad-leafed native shrub. "I'll leave the reason why to your imagination." After pointing out dozens of unusual plants, for each of which he seemed to have an anecdote, he concluded with a mischievous grin, "There are a lot of young designers now who don't know the difference between a dandelion and a daisy."

Reluctantly bidding the Colliers farewell, we continued southward toward the coastal city of Napier. The next item on our itinerary read: "Before entering Napier, enjoy a tour of Trelinnoe Park." This had to be the understatement of the tour, for the place turned out to be one of the most remarkable private gardens I've ever seen. I speak here as a tree person, for Trelinnoe is a "Garden of Landscape," according to its owners, John and Fiona Wills. While operating a 2,500-acre sheep and cattle ranch with their sons and John's brother, this amazing pair have found time to create a 30-acre woodland garden of exquisite taste and sophistication. As John explained, one of the glories of gardening in New Zealand is that the accelerated growth rate allows you to plant a tree and live to see it become a mature specimen. He's planted 250 magnolias, many now sixty-six feet or more high. An oval with a huge pin oak at its center is surrounded by a circle of lawn and an outer circle of copper beeches underplanted with massed blue hydrangeas. Then, on through grove after grove of rare and exotic trees and shrubs, many grown from seed from various parts of Asia and the Americas, all planted with an eye for complementary textures and the play of light through leaves. As he marched along purposefully, John casually produced dozens upon dozens of botanical names, many for species we'd never heard of. At one point a name eluded him momentarily, and he bemoaned how the brain slows down with age.

John regaled us equally with plant names and gardening wisdom. Under an enormous eucalyptus, he shook his head. "Eucalyptus trees have no sense of gravity—they put their branches out and out, and then down the whole works comes." Recent pruning had him reflecting: "They say with gardening you start with the spade and end with the chain saw." Gazing up through the foliage of several *Acer hookeri* planted on a knoll, he mused that "texture and light are the fundamentals of garden design." For that reason, he said, standing in an oval of clipped beech, "I did my planning at dawn and dusk, for sunlight behind the foliage." At "the Moonwatch," a variegated dogwood stretched horizontally, picking up the lines of hills in the far distance. "We come down here in the evening to watch the moon rise over the hills, a ball of orange," John explained. Near the end he led us to the "Vista of Earth and Sky"—an expanse of lawn sweeping uphill with only vivid blue sky visible at its crest. "A nice way to end the garden," he said as we climbed the gentle slope, "is to walk into the sky and into infinity." After rambling for four hours through this leafy tour de force, we left exhausted and exhilarated.

"Oh, you'll love the South Island," people on the North Island kept telling us. "The people are much friendlier down there, and the farther south you go, the friendlier they get." And the more British they get, too, or at least their gardens do. Having flown south, we stopped in the old gold-mining community of Arrowtown to visit Kathleen Fleck, whose gorgeous little cottage garden was done in a very English way with hostas, roses, clematis, lilies, hollyhocks, sweet peas, peonies, pelargoniums, and all the rest. As we were leaving, she told us we really should drop in at her friend Elizabeth's garden, around the corner. We found Elizabeth Knox working in her yard, a steep hillside with a traditional-style cottage perched on its top. A slender little person eighty-nine years old, she started this garden when she was seventy-seven and still maintained it by herself. Her daughter liked to tease her that she had one leg longer than the other from working on the hill. "I've enjoyed it up to this point," she told us with a smile, "but I'm getting too old for it." You wanted her to live, and keep gardening, forever just the way she was.

One of the great delights of touring the New Zealand countryside, particularly on the South Island, is experiencing the tussock grasslands, where persistent winds comb through vast expanses of tall, tawny grasses, creating a landscape of rippling beauty. The high hill grasslands are dominated by snow grasses, which have large tussocks and often tall, stout, flowering stems. All are members of an indigenous genus called *Chionochloa,* several of whose two dozen species are cultivated in gardens, none to my mind more pleasingly than the red tussock, *C. rubra.* Spreading almost six and a half feet wide and nearly as tall, its fine, reddish foliage tosses in the wind like the tresses of an earthy supermodel. *Chionochloa conspicua* is lovely, too, waving its multiple feathery flower heads.

Another group of native tall tussocks are called toetoe. These are cortaderia and look like refined forms of pampas grass. They are relatives of the South American native, but there the resemblance ends, for whereas native tussock grasses have been severely reduced in their range through development, the introduced pampas grass has become an aggressive invader, as have Chilean gunnera and agapanthus from South Africa. Many a North American gardener has gone to an early grave from frustrated attempts to cultivate one or other of these, to Kiwis, "undesirable organisms." More desirable by far, some of the native New Zealand sedges rival the tussock grasses for attractiveness in the garden. *Carex testacea* and *C. flagellifera* are two bronze beauties we saw widely planted, most effectively in large groupings. *Carex secta,* an expansive, water-loving sedge, grows gracefully alongside large ponds, as at Ayrlies, and on the banks of the Avon River in Christchurch.

And it was in that very "Garden City" we'd structured the tour to climax, during the annual "Flowers & Romance Festival—Petals, Passion, Possibilities." Oh, my. Taking the high road, I shall dwell only upon the festival's singular triumph, a "Romance of the Seasons" Wearable Flowers Parade in Christchurch Cathedral. The half-hour show featured ballet dancers parading down a runway and modeling "wearable flower costumes" designed and created by Christchurch fabric artist Jenny Gillies. The costumes were ingenious, each one a different flower, perhaps an enormous silken peony or jaunty fuchsia or a rose nodding from the bowed head of the model. The elegance of the dancers, the brilliance of the costumes, with classical music playing and shafts of sunlight slanting through the cathedral's stained glass windows—as an ecclesiastical experience this was a vast leap forward from the morbid pulpit-pounding of my youth.

The gardens we visited in and around Christchurch all lived up to the city's floral reputation. I especially enjoyed Millstream Garden north of the city, out on the flat and windswept Canterbury Plain. Enormous hedges planted as windbreaks are a feature of the countryside, and a mania for hedging has swept into many of the region's gardens. Such is the case with Elaine and John Lynn. After purchasing five acres of bare paddock fifteen years ago, the first thing they did was plant a shelterbelt around the property. Geometric hedging eventually became the defining motif of the garden.

Almost every Kiwi gardener we met seemed to have some variation on the same garden-starting theme. "No, there was nothing here, just a bare paddock, when we started fifteen years ago," they told us. Their trees were enormous, their shrubberies bulging fulsomely, their perennial borders longer than an elephant's memory. "Oh, yes, we did all the work ourselves," they said jauntily, "after work or on weekends, y'know." I was repeatedly beating back the sensation that we'd been spinning our wheels at home while these New Zealand zealots had created masterpieces in half the time.

Millstream Garden is an extreme case in point. Created from Elaine's impeccable horticultural instincts, its design is elegantly formal, with hedge-lined walks and avenues and distinct garden rooms. The alder walk, for example, is a long, grassy sward enclosed by macrocarpa hedges, within which twin rows of evergreen alders are underplanted with hebes. It's simple, uncluttered, and stunningly beautiful. Throughout the garden there are hedges of box and macrocarpa, purple berberis, pittosporum, and clipped beech. An escallonia hedge combines with fastigiate macrocarpa and silver pear trees behind. And topiary everywhere. A banker by trade and espalierist at heart, John is a man called to clip. This is no wealthy banker's garden, in which hired hands do the heavy lifting; true gardeners, John and Elaine do the grunt labor themselves. They compost old leaves and grass clippings and spread 130 bales of pea straw for mulch each year. "I love making things," Elaine laughed. "I love the concrete mixer!"

Such was the spirit of vigorous, hands-on workaholism we encountered over and over again in this gardening-mad little country. After the tour ended, Sandy and I spent another month exploring the South Island by car. Imagine impossibly romantic evenings tenting on the shores of the Tasman Sea, a warm breeze blowing, the Southern Cross high above us in a night sky glittering with unknown constellations. In another location we were pricked awake by a very spiny little hedgehog, who insisted on snuggling up with us under the tent. A different campground offered a midnight attack by outlaw opossums and a daytime Wild West cattle drive right through the camp. Caves and rivers and sadly remnant rain forests and, shimmering on the horizon, the magnificent Southern Alps. And more gardens, of course, always more gardens born of the passionate zeal of New Zealand's masterful gardeners.

Garden Artistry

I<small>T IS MOST</small> desirable that the garden be a garden, so that its manager may get on with the necessary propagations, fertilizations, and other preoccupations. By some immutable law, these activities are always more than sufficient to consume whatever time is available. But this garden as garden is not to be. Rather than doing something useful, such as pleaching the limes or liming the beds for rutabagas, the gardener is repeatedly dragged indoors for interminable discussions concerning garden artistry. Is the garden a true work of art? Should the gardener be thought of as an artist, every bit the aesthetic equal of the sculptor or the composer? Are we gardeners—too long associated with shuffling underlings on great estates—failing to hold our heads sufficiently high in the arena of artistic achievement?

The world of High Art is plainly less than enthusiastic about throwing open its doors to hordes of guileless gardeners. I mean, where would you draw the line? Surely you wouldn't mount Aunt Tilly's hanging baskets on the same pedestal as Warhol's Campbell's Soup can? Your neighbor Fred's display of calla lilies may be drop-dead gorgeous, but is it in the same league as a chichi gallery showing of 382 old microwave ovens artfully stacked inside encircling razor wire? No, it is not, nor can it ever be, because the imprisoned microwaves make a statement, profoundly disturbing though it may be, about the human condition, whereas Fred's callas can speak only of callas. Viewed from the plinth of High Art, the most inane assemblage of objets trouvés, installed in a gallery for two weeks, will garner far greater acclaim than will a nearby garden, no matter how sophisticated and enduring its design. A slender volume of poems so impenetrable they'll be read by at most half a dozen semi-demented university professors can capture a Governor General's Award, whereas a garden that delights and inspires thousands, for generations, gets no official recognition whatsoever.

Most gardeners, like becalmed Buddhists, simply accept that this is what is. But certain horticultural social climbers are not about to be so offhandedly discounted. They take their cue from the likes of Alexander Pope—or was it his less-oft-quoted contemporary, William Kent?—who declared, "All gardening is landscape painting." Seconding the motion, acclaimed landscape designer Roberto Burle Marx wrote: "A garden is a complex of aesthetic and plastic intentions; and the plant is, to a landscape artist, not only a plant—rare, unusual, ordinary or doomed to disappearance—but it is also a color, a shape, a volume or an arabesque in itself." So there you are: not some grubby laborer up to your gum boots in pig shit after all, but an artist, painting living landscapes by means of arabesques.

A harmless enough conceit, you might suppose; but in the real world, prying into the question of garden artistry pops the lid off a Pandora's box of problems. The pressures from great expectations can be crushing, the opportunities for miscalculation immeasurable. Clearing out the attic some while ago, for example, I unearthed several long-forgotten treasures. Two of them, an old butter churn and an ornate, hand-cranked cream separator, were throwbacks to the days when Sandy and I kept milk goats on the place. These relics had lain in the attic for the better part of two decades, and I saw no reason why they shouldn't remain there indefinitely. Sandy, however, had other ideas. "I think we should use them as garden art," she proposed. I felt an instinctive tightening of the intestines at this suggestion. To my way of thinking, treasures like the cream separator are best stored safely away for a future time at which their antique value will have risen so dizzyingly that their sale will more than offset any negligence there may have been in getting a realistic pension plan in place. The garden artist eschews such seamy practicality, preferring to scatter old collectibles around the yard, blithely indifferent to the likelihood of their disintegration. In this diversity of outlook hoarders are no match for garden artists, as hoarding is by nature a venal, vaguely shameful behavior, whereas garden artistry betokens a carefree and extravagant lightness of spirit.

Even the most stubbornly inartistic among us find our resistance weakening whenever we encounter the gardens of accomplished artistes—gardens remarkable for brilliant touches: clusters of sticks, each painted a vivid color; boulders splashed with paint or wrapped in raffia; swaths of colored silks suspended from overhanging boughs. At every turn, in every glade, something too terribly clever. But thought-provoking, too. Iconic in some vague but stirring way. Mythic, like all great art. How do they manage it? you wonder. "Oh, we could do something like that!" your companion enthuses. And we do. Or at least we try. We've created little spills of broken crockery, seashells, bits of coral, and shining stones brought home from expeditions abroad. Several wooden carpenters' boxes bulge with antique hand tools. (Perfectly serviceable hand tools, actually, pilfered from my tool shed). A gang of merry plastic clowns peeps out from under a hydrangea. An ancient metal hand plow stands nestled against a clump of *Romneya coulteri*. We're not presumptuous enough to refer to such oddments as Art, but they may be safely catalogued as "artistic touches."

Occasionally, one does draw tantalizingly close to the high altar of Art. A Japanese maple that died an inexplicable death, as Japanese maples are wont to do, was trimmed of its lesser twigs and had its trunk and limbs painted a vivid blue, which picks up the nearby flowers of blue anchusa and the mophead hydrangeas behind. A desaturated lavender veil drapes over an arm of the maple as though Isadora Duncan were flirting with the flowers of a nearby *Magnolia x soulangeana*. The entire composition is so frightfully artful we're inclined to preen about it in front of our ceramic-artist and fiber-artist friends. But a singular success such as this doesn't ensure a successful successor. Nearby sits what some have come to think of as "Imelda's Folly"—a row of old boots arrayed along the seat of a bench, each pair painted gold or white or blue and each with a cluster of silk flowers growing out of it. It has been much photographed. It has been featured in the local newspaper. But is it Art or just a quirky curiosity? Would it be more artful if the boots were wrapped in razor wire?

The difficulty with not being a garden artist oneself is that one never knows whether a particular installation is High Art or just tacky bric-a-brac guaranteed to elicit a smirk from aesthetically elevated observers. People like Oscar Wilde, who opined that bad art is a great deal worse than no art at all. Genuine garden artists make the distinction instinctively, but the rest of us are compelled to grope through the dark, like moles. We may be clear enough about mass-produced garden ornaments of the gnomes-holding-fishing-poles genre, but is an antique wheelbarrow intrinsically tacky or not? Uncertain, you may conceal it behind the *Maclea cordata,* whereas a confident garden artist will paint the old barrow a bold yellow and have massed nasturtiums breaking over it in a frothy wave of brilliant color. How chic! Not to be left behind in any artsy wheelbarrow race, we have a barrow of our own—a crumbling metal one in whose bucket our resident garden artist has placed a large mirror with costume jewelry scattered over it. A similar avidity inspired the suspending of multiple small glitter balls from the branches of a cork tree, so that on sunny days reflected sunlight dances in tiny splashes through the house. And, by way of a *pièce de résistance à la glitter,* we've hung over the patio a mass of contorted Harry Lauder's walking stick prunings clustered with golden, silver, and crystal ornaments.

These installations lack the measure of safety provided by more practical garden ornaments—a Lutyens bench or Jekyll pots. But even here, gray areas loom: Is an authentic replica windmill with no mill attached really a thing of beauty? Can any good come of a wishing well with no well? As in the art world generally, such aesthetic quandaries can be covered over with a mulch of money. An Italian wellhead in pink Istrian stone will, even without a well underneath, never suffer the slights endured by a fake rustic wishing well. It helps enormously if the goods are imported. Moorish tiles, Mediterranean birdbaths, Etruscan urns, and old Provençal garden vases are all safe bets. Or you can stick your well-heeled foot into the doorway of High Art and refuse to withdraw it, by creating an impressionist courtyard or scattering cubist blocks across the lawn.

Those of us with a limited line of credit might do best to adopt an all-or-nothing approach to garden accessories. Either have none of them, instead relying upon the inherent beauty of our plantings, or give the yard over entirely to ornament. Taken to its extreme, the mania for garden collectibles leaps beyond the limitations of High Art, surmounts the outlying boundaries of tackiness, and enters the Elysian fields of kitsch, the dominant art form of our times. You will find many of its most ardent devotees living in waterfront homes, where the yard is a seething miasma of gnarled driftwood pieces, glass floats, bleached whale bones, peculiarly shaped stones, and fragments of old machineries. There may be a few miserable plants peeping out from under the debris, but gardening plainly takes a backseat.

No matter how tastefully installed, ornamentation cannot compare with garden artistry in its most elevated form. I refer to the exalted art of topiary, the shaping of plants by pruning, tying, and shearing them into nonnatural forms. Great art picks up where nature ends, Marc Chagall maintained, and what art form hangs with more exquisite grace upon the very verge of nature than does the art of the topiarist?

His is an ancient profession whose popularity has waxed and waned over the centuries, contributing to many of history's greatest gardens as well as to some of horticulture's most grotesque excesses. Amid the splendor of imperial Rome, Pliny the Younger wrote enthusiastically of his *gestatio* in Tuscany, "laid out in the form of a circus running round the multiform box-hedge and the dwarf-trees, which are cut quite close. The whole is fenced in with a wall completely covered by box cut into steps all the way up to the top." Box-edged paths and elaborate topiary were a mainstay of the great villa gardens of the Italian Renaissance. During the sixteenth century, enthusiasm for the "antike worke" of hedge and shrub carving made its way from Italy into the estate gardens of France and the Netherlands and from there to Tudor England. These "gardens of curiosities" were all the rage in the Elizabethan age and continued to hold sway for several centuries. The English mania for shearing trees and shrubs into fantastic shapes culminated in the seventeenth-century "Dutch" garden at Levens Hall in Westmoreland, which became the most renowned topiary garden in the world. Its French designer, Guillaume Beaumont, who had been trained under André Le Nôtre at Versailles and who had laid out the gardens at Hampton Court, created an outlandish landscape of enormous spirals, globules, cake stands, and geometric oddities. But then came the crash. With the rise of romanticism in the eighteenth century and the new, naturalistic "landscape style" of gardening, topiary became a laughingstock. Alexander Pope—he of the landscape painting—mercilessly mocked the form, deriding "Adam and Eve in yew," "Saint George in box," "Queen Elizabeth in myrtle," and "a lavender pig with sage growing in his belly." After centuries of greatness, topiary was unequivocally "out." And out it would remain, save for occasional brave sorties by maladjusted Victorian aristocrats. It was referred to as "almost a lost art."

But mark the "almost," because today topiary's soaring toward the top once again. Glossy new books on the art abound. Topiary nurseries stand ready to supply a wide variety of completed specimens. For dopey topiarists, "artificial" and "synthetic" topiary specimens are available too. A plethora of topiary gifts and products await purchase. Topiary tours may be taken. Strangely (much of topiary involves strangeness), one of the great champions of this long-awaited renaissance is the Disney entertainment empire. Back in the 1960s Walt himself initiated the use of topiary in the first Disneyland park in California. Unconcerned with the niceties of High Art, Disney had his film animators collaborate with the Disneyland landscaping department to create a topiary Dumbo the Elephant, dancing hippos from *Fantasia,* and similar crowd-pleasers. The tradition has continued, and today the Walt Disney World Resort in Florida is like a contemporary Levens Hall, boasting hundreds of topiary shapes including giraffes and camels, polar bears and podocarpus sea serpents. There's an *Ilex vomitoria* Mary Poppins holding a *Pyracantha coccinea* umbrella, and a holly elephant dances on a striped beach ball of alternanthera. You can just imagine Pope's withering scorn at encountering Goofy in pyracantha.

On a perhaps more appealing scale, one may suddenly come upon the handiwork of a confirmed topiarist while wandering down a country lane or through a city suburb. My heart always soars at the sight, for I have an abiding passion for topiary. Shamelessly, I adore clipped yews, sheared box, and shaped bay. Despite espousing noble ideals concerning native and wildlife-friendly plants, I nurture a perverse fascination with clipping helpless evergreens into pyramids, globes, and cones. Though our garden lacks dancing hippos, I derive inordinate satisfaction from one little composition featuring a clipped pyramidal dwarf Alberta spruce alongside an upright rectangle of English yew and a pair of globular western red huckleberries. This latter element—shearing even defenseless native shrubs into geometric objects—graphically illustrates the excesses of enthusiasm that can debase the topiarist's art.

But it is an art nevertheless, requiring the eye of both artist and sculptor to visualize the desired shapes and encourage plants into that form. It involves, as one writer put it, a fascinating blend of clairvoyance, draftsmanship, and silviculture. And a touch of madness. Because the limitations and the hazards are considerable. Choice of shape, for example. "The conventional shapes are as standard as those of formal heraldry," warns British writer Tyler Whittle, "and it takes nerves and a sure touch to experiment with subjects outside the list." Simple geometric forms—globes and cones and all the rest—are by far the easiest to execute, and they avoid any of the hazards of venturing beyond the coda. Our place is littered with spherical yews and berberis, globular dwarf spruce and hollies, rotund boxes and portly huckleberries. On a bad day the garden looks like the Jolly Green Giant's bowling alley. I currently have my eye on an innocent little Japanese holly, upon which I intend to perform the ancient art of Japanese cloud pruning; sinuous stems are stripped bare of their leaves and shaped to terminate in a poof of foliage, somewhat like the clipping certain poodles are forced to endure.

One drawback to the business is the amount of time required to execute a topnotch topiary. No Jackson Pollocks permitted here, splashing their paint maniacally, then dashing off to the next canvas. The aphorism is that gardening is the slowest of the performing arts. The topiarist must sometimes wait decades for the full realization of a triumph. I remember gasping with delight at Powerscourt Estate in Ireland upon encountering a compact evergreen—it may have been a dwarf Alberta spruce—that had been sheared over the years to perfectly resemble the peak of Sugarloaf Mountain in the distance.

The topiary artist also expends enormous amounts of time and effort in *keeping* shapes meticulously sheared. There are few sights more dispiriting than a topiary giraffe sprouting scruffy shoots. Unfortunately, as with the gardener generally, the topiarist tends to bite off more than he can decently chew. The leafy geometries at our place exist in a perpetual state of near-frowziness, as my shearing invariably proceeds at a slower clip than the one at which plants grow. As befits a true artist, I employ only hand tools, primarily an antique pair of wooden-handled hedge clippers that I picked up at the Denman Island

Free Store. An electric hedge trimmer would allow me to keep pace more efficiently, but I feel strongly that resorting to such a convenience would debase my art to the level of persons using chain saws to carve logs into the shape of grizzly bears. Far worse than a bit of scruffiness, shrubs too ardently sheared—a particular hazard of electric trimmers—may suffer also from the dreaded "brown out." The bane of the topiarist is dieback on a branch critical to the sculpture or, worse, death of the whole plant.

Notwithstanding the difficulties of the form or the scorn of unenlightened gardeners, not to mention blatant sneering from bona fide artistes, we topiarists persist, dreaming of the day when this venerable art form will be once again appropriately appreciated. As a certain W. Gibson, former head gardener at the remarkable Levens Hall, once wrote: "Topiary Work although greatly neglected, and in many cases largely despised, has a future before it; of that we are certain, so long as the art is kept within reasonable limits and not foolishly overdone. By many modern gardeners it is always referred to as a monument of perverted taste, but we hope that this obviously unjust appellation may soon be withdrawn."

How prophetic his words, for the unjust appellation is even now crumbling before us, as are the fortifications of High Art itself. For proof we need look no farther than Columbus, Ohio, where there exists in a downtown park the only known topiary interpretation of a painting. Created in 1992, the topiary park recreates Georges

Seurat's famous Post-Impressionist painting *Sunday Afternoon on the Island of La Grande Jatte*. Fifty-four topiary people populate the piece, along with three leafy dogs, one cat, and one monkey. The park is hailed as a "landscape of a painting of a landscape." Its sparkling triple play trumps vile detractors of the topiarist's art, while making a brilliant statement about the consummate artistry of gardening. So set aside your razor wire, and let's hear a warm round of applause for all true artists of the garden.

The Seven Deadly Sins

RAISED AS I was in a staunchly religious Irish Catholic family, and having had the church's eternal options of redemption and damnation polished to a gleaming luminosity during my eight years as a seminarian with the hellfire-preaching Passionist Fathers, I retain, these many decades later, some lingering affinity with moral rectitude. As a youth, I'd conclude each day with an examination of conscience whereby any transgression, impiety, or evil deed I'd committed would be identified; forgiveness would be sought from above before surrendering to a sleep from which I might never awaken. Saturday invariably entailed a trip to the confessional, where I knelt in the dark enclosure and whispered my sins to the listening priest, was cross-examined on any salacious bits, and was then absolved and released, filled with a firm, if unrealistic, purpose to go and sin no more.

That once solid bedrock of confession and absolution is much eroded with the passage of time, but not sufficiently to dissuade me from proposing a contemplation of the Seven Deadly Sins of Gardening—and the possibilities of redemption to be found in their corresponding Seven Contrary Virtues.

We begin with the first, and arguably worst, of the seven deadly sins, the sin from which the other six in this vile litter spring. Namely, the sin of Pride. Yes: pride, vanity, the high or overweaning opinion of one's own qualities, attainments, or estate. Vanity of vanities, all is vanity. But right from the outset we run into difficulty in trying to distinguish between loathsome pride and simple acceptance of reality. Because, actually, one's own garden is undeniably superior to almost every other that one encounters. The awkward but inescapable truth remains that one is a far more accomplished gardener than most other people, though a bit of discretion is called for in not trumpeting this obvious fact too loudly.

No, in discussing pride, we're not talking about the self-satisfaction of genuinely superior gardeners, but rather of an arrogant minority who flaunt themselves in a most disagreeable way. "Yes, we're really rather pleased," the prideful gardener announces while showing you around her estate. "Now, just look over there—you'll notice how the *Scabiosa caucasica* Clive Greaves, the *Lavandula spica,* the *Clematis ascotiensis,* and the *Solanum crispum* Glasnevin are all muted violet or purple blues, their color enhanced by gray santolina beneath them and the gray hardscape beyond." You might not have noticed this if she hadn't pointed it out, but you never have to worry about prideful gardeners being stuck for something to say. They've always got something to say, and it's always about themselves or their wonderful gardens. "Isn't that just the most charming little *Erigeron karvinskianus* you've ever laid eyes on?" they exclaim. "And do come see my helianthemum Wisely Pink—it's by far the grandest specimen you're likely to ever encounter." These braggarts have always got the choicest varieties of everything, in the cleverest combinations, and shown to best effect.

The real problem here is, as much as you hate to admit it, the gardens created by these peacocks are splendid, perfect, impeccable. Their agapanthus are pantingly blue and beautiful, picking up the metallic-blue pods hanging between elegant green leaves of a *Decaisnea fargesii*. Their foliage frameworks are magnificent, their color plans extraordinary. And it's for that reason that you never, ever want to invite them over to see your garden. They'll glance around your yard with an expression of dismay. "Ah, yes, well," they'll say, "you've made a very brave start, haven't you? You must have the heart of a lion to tackle a place like this." They won't have been paying attention when you told them you've been gardening here for twenty years. "But look, once you get rid of all this garish clutter"—they'll dismiss your prized perennial bed with a wave—"you'll have room to bring in some really interesting plants, won't you?" Left unchecked, their vanity will spill over into out-right effrontery. "Oh, good Lord!" they'll exclaim, "surely you're not allowing that dreadful *Fatsia japonica* to stay there? No, as much as it hurts me to say it, it's all wrong. This unfortunate euphorbia with the griselinia and hypericum—no, I'm sorry, I just can't bear to look at it!"

Beneath these outbursts the message is always the same: My garden is better than your garden, and I know more about gardening than you do. I can demonstrate as much by dazzling you with my knowledge of botanical Latin. You may think that's a fennel plant you've got over there, but I would never call it by any other name than *Foeniculum vulgare*. Rather than 'toad lily,' which sounds so inelegant, I far prefer to say *Tricyrtis formosana*. And really, I ask you, how could anyone employ a vulgarism like 'Russian sage' when one really means *Perovskia atriplicifolia*?

The whole time, you're biting your tongue to keep from saying that you yourself prefer to call *Saxifraga urbium* by its common name: London pride. But we don't say anything, do we? We're meek as lambs in the face of this appalling vanity, aren't we? That's because we're trying our best to practice the virtue contrary to Pride: Humility. Sweet *Humilitas*. The holding of a low opinion of oneself. It is within these cramped and modest quarters that we find most gardeners. A visit to the garden of the humble gardener provokes a litany of self-recrimination and apology. "Well, it's not much to look at right now," we grovel, in front of whoever's come to visit. "Things are in a bit of a mess at the moment. I'm sorry for all the clutter—we just haven't gotten around to cleaning things up yet." The humble gardener darts about, plucking out weeds and kicking heaps of rubbish off the pathways. "Oh, don't look over there—that border's a disaster at the moment! My Lord, the winterkill this year took a dreadful toll. And the breakage from those heavy snowfalls—catastrophic! Good grief, that dogwood doesn't look very happy, does it? And, oh, no!—the roots of that berberis are exposed again. It's never going to make it through summer."

Everywhere the humble gardener looks, misfortune looms. "I cannot believe I planted that deutzia right there! Right there among the callicarpa? I mean, what was I possibly thinking? And look here: the clematis and roses are so tangled together, you can't prune either one of them properly. Oh, Lord, some days I think we should tear the whole garden out and start over again." Caution is advisable, though, since humility may begin to degenerate into unseemly self-loathing. "Oh, I'll never have a green thumb, no matter how long I stay at it. Nothing ever seems to work for me. Everything I plant dies." And finally, humiliatingly, "I think my plants all hate me!" Lashing herself long and hard, the contrite gardener becomes the horticultural equivalent of Mel Gibson's Jesus.

Fortunately, many gardeners find an escape from the twin perils of vanity and self-debasement. The escape route is that lovely middle ground known to gardeners everywhere: false modesty. "Well, it's not much to look at yet, really," we tell our friends as we survey the new rockery and scree we've just put in, even though in our heart of hearts we know it's the cleverest thing since Einstein. "But a couple of years from now, when things have grown in a bit, it probably won't look too bad." The falsely modest gardener intends these lines as a cue for the visitor to insist the opposite is true. But eliciting the proper response is no simple matter. The arrogant garden visitor will agree that the place isn't much to look at. Visiting humility freaks will fawn embarrassingly over your rockery and scree. "Oh, it's so beautiful," they'll simper. "It's the most beautiful thing I ever saw. I could never do something like that; I'm such a klutz. How do you manage it? Do you think you could come over to my place and give me some pointers?"

Neither of these extremes constitutes a satisfactory response. All you require is for someone to acknowledge the genius of your creation and say simply: "You know, that is a brilliant bit of work." But will anyone do that? No. And the reason why is to be found in the second of the seven deadly sins: Envy. Yes, filthy envy. To regard with discontent another person's possession of some superior advantage. To wish oneself on a level with another in some respect, or possessed of something that another person has. It occurs to me that perhaps we speak of people being "green with envy" because this one, of all the deadly sins, seems to have particular appeal to gardeners. We look at another garden not so much to delight in the pleasures it may offer but rather to compare it with our own. And in the comparing, to find reasons why this garden, which at first glance might appear more distinguished than our own, really isn't.

"Well, look at the advantages these people have," we grumble. "They've obviously got a great little microclimate in here. Southwest exposure. Wonderful sunshine. Protection from the southeasters. And two feet of rich, sandy loam to start with. All the water in the world. I mean, any idiot could grow a good garden here. And the money these people keep lavishing on this place. They've obviously come into a substantial inheritance, and if you or I had half as much cash to throw around, we'd do twice as well as they have with it."

We raise our own trees from seed, of course, so that fifteen years later they're still only three feet high, but these nouveau riche buy enormous trees from a specialty nursery and have them installed by crews with big machinery. Well, come on now, where's the real gardening in that? Rather than making their own compost heaps like we do, from kitchen scraps and canary droppings, they have a truck arrive every week with a load of well-rotted alpaca manure from friends of theirs out in the valley. Naturally, if we had a state-of-the-art greenhouse like theirs, with computerized moisture and temperature control, we'd be able to raise perfect seedlings too, instead of the wizened little runts we raise on our bathroom window ledge. And who'd want their poncy collection of rare orchids and tropical epiphytes, anyway?

These people have a parade of professional helpers trooping into the place to do their work for them. While you're out there pruning and shearing and making a go of it on your own, they have a topiarist in to clip their hedges, an arborist to prune their trees, a rosarian to tend their roses, and an espalierist to train their fruit. What an intrusion, having those hordes tramping around the place all the time. Plus, you'd far rather have the satisfaction of doing the work yourself. Just imagine what you could do with all that beautiful flagstone they hired someone to lay down. And naturally they have to have the most gorgeous pool and cascade in the world, with absolutely no algae, and no layer of sludge at the bottom like there always is in your little sunken plastic pool. No herons or raccoons ever come over and eat their goldfish. They don't have squirrels digging up their bulbs or neighborhood cats defecating in their seedbeds. I mean, everything these people have is perfect, isn't it? Perfectly perfect. They spend the afternoon playing croquet on the lawn and sipping chilled mint tea in a pergola dripping with aromatic honeysuckle and jasmine, while you're out covered with sweat and soil, fighting to the death with malicious creeping buttercup.

But are you the least bit envious of these arrivistes? Certainly not! You wouldn't trade your garden for theirs. Your garden is so hands-on, so down-to-earth, so authentic. You wouldn't want a garish display garden like theirs, not in a million years. And you certainly wouldn't want to be hailed far and wide as a marvelous gardener and have your place photographed for chic gardening magazines and calendars and have your advice constantly sought in high-toned discussions of garden design. Absolutely not. Still, it is odd, isn't it, how when one looks in the mirror after visiting their place, one's complexion seems to have turned an unpleasant shade of green.

The virtue contrary to Envy is Love, the ability to look upon others with affectionate and tender consideration. "Charity suffereth long, and is kind; charity envieth not," says Saint Paul. Where envy resents the good things others receive, love actively seeks the good of others. "Thou shalt love thy neighbor as thyself." You almost certainly would if only you had a better class of neighbor to deal with. But that bunch of yobs across the back fence with the three vicious Rottweilers—I don't think so. And the guy next door with the world-class sound system for playing his Barry Manilow CDs over and over again. Arrrgggh! No, you wouldn't love that bunch of losers for love or for money.

It's for this very reason, I believe, that so many gardeners come in due course to see love as something better directed toward plants. "My love is like a red, red rose!" the lovesome gardener coos. Proudly, we call our garden "a labor of love." Tenderly we cultivate our love-in-a-mist, our love-lies-bleeding, love-in-idleness, love-bind, and the love tree. The more randy among us call our tomatoes "love apples." We speak unabashedly about the ability of plants to love. "Yes, the violet loves a sunny bank," we'll say. "The hosta loves a bit of shade." Excessively emotive companion planters speak endlessly of "tomatoes loving garlic" and all the rest.

Gradually, insidiously, the love-struck gardener comes to believe that she is in an intimate relationship with her plants. She is convinced that her plants are capable of reciprocal affection, that they have tender feelings toward her. She begins talking to her babies. She encourages them to get well, to grow, to thrive. Eventually, she imagines the plants are talking back to her, whispering their greeny secret love. Not unreasonably, she concludes that most plants are far more intelligent than most people. That plants are lovely in and of themselves. She wanders the garden enchanted, languishing, as Dryden writes, "Where nightingales their love-sick ditty sing."

But suddenly the Rottweilers are lunging and snarling, Barry Manilow reaches a thundering crescendo on "Can't Smile Without You," and all love's lost, to be instantly replaced by the third deadly sin—Anger. Anger, that boiling stew of indignation, intense exasperation, and resentment. Rage.

Now I daresay that most people in the world think of gardeners as mild creatures, maybe even a bit airy-fairy, and certainly not given to angry outbursts. We think of road rage, air rage, hockey rage, but does anyone acknowledge that there's such a thing as garden rage? Although it remains a dirty little secret, all gardeners know that the wrath of Jehovah, the biblical day of wrath and fury, is an insignificant poof! compared with a full-blown blast of garden rage.

Consider the provocations. You start off on a lovely sunny morning in a state of delightsome equanimity, only to discover that damping-off has withered most of your tomato seedlings. Your spirit somewhat dampened, you next realize to your horror that nocturnal slugs have demolished your broccoli transplants. Looking up, you see that there are dozens of tent caterpillar nests in the cherry trees. Things continue to go from bad to worse when you realize that thieving crows have dug up your corn seeds and sow bugs are eating your strawberries. You feel a definite jolt of resentment at the cankers growing like tumors on the rose canes. Clubroot's killing the cabbages, and root maggots have gotten the rutabagas. Resentment rises to exasperation when you notice that the clematis are wilting. Again. The wisteria has mysteriously succumbed to sudden vine death syndrome. And the kids next door have just smashed your greenhouse with a baseball. Vexation mounts as a sudden hailstorm slashes your hostas to tatters. Your monkshood are down on their knees. Raccoons have stolen your grapes, and your lawn's got more dandelions and moss than grass. Vexation ratchets up to indignation that there are starlings in your swallow boxes and squirrels raiding your bird feeder. The bats won't use your bat house, and the orchard mason bees won't go near your orchard mason bee holes. Indignation turns to ire when your dear companion tells you that the tree you spent all day yesterday planting is six inches too close to the driveway. The clay pots you left out last winter have cracked, and the water line has sprung a leak. Anger begins to boil over as you discover the pool holds hundreds of thousands of mosquito larvae, each of which is probably carrying West Nile virus. The rose arbor's listing precariously, and the tomatoes all have blossom-end rot. Anger erupts into wrath because the sweet-pea trellis has toppled. And that goddamn sapsucker's back, drilling holes in the trunk of your mountain ash tree! Wrath becomes rage when you slice your finger again with the bloody secateurs. And rage morphs to fury when the deer get in overnight and demolish the whole damn garden. Like mad King Lear, you stand amid the devastation and roar with fiercely righteous indignation. *Rooaarrr!!!*

This is what we mean by garden rage. But, as I say, the world beyond the garden gates has no idea that gardeners are regularly provoked to a wrath that would terrify the likes of Todd Bertuzzi. No, our public image is entirely the opposite, manifesting the contrary virtue to Anger—Kindness. It is perhaps contemporary gardening's supreme achievement, this clever spin-doctoring by which we have managed to convince a gullible public that we gardeners are naturally genial beings, sympathetic, courteous, dripping with benevolence. They picture us contentedly puttering in our gardens, a joyful smile upon our lips, butterflies and songbirds fluttering beside us, while we hum a little ditty to ourselves:

> Life is mostly froth and bubble
> Two things stand like stone—
> Kindness in another's trouble
> Courage in our own.

I say let the public retain their romantic fantasies concerning fey gardeners, pixies and nosegays, and pretty pressed flowers. Better this than the alternative—that outsiders discover how the jack-booted troops of horticulture behave behind those carefully clipped hedges. Anger is not the only thing that gardeners strive to keep hidden from public view. There's the fourth of the Seven Deadly Sins of Gardening, as well: Avarice. Greed. Cupidity. The desire to get and hoard wealth. "Greed is good," they say on Wall Street, and society has come to accept this crazed capitalist chant. Sociopathic greed we now label as success. But the avarice of the investment banker or insider trader or junk bond pirate is child's play, penny-ante trifling, compared with the monstrous green greed of the gardener. The love of money may drive disgraced CEOs caught in accounting scandals, but none is more unscrupulous or more miserly than the avaricious gardener.

"I simply must have a *Vanda Rothschildiana,* or I'll die," the greedy gardener says with a steely look in her eye.

"I've got three hundred different roses at my place," says another, "but I won't be happy till I've got five hundred."

"I've planted over two thousand rhododendrons in my woods," somebody else chips in, "and I've only gotten started."

These chronic acquirers need a special software program on their computers just to tabulate how many plants they have. Walking through somebody else's garden with one of them can be mortifying. "Yes, I've got that," she'll say. "Got those, got those." She ticks off each plant you pass, as though they were car parts on a warehouse shelf. "Have a more elegant variety of that. Wouldn't bother with that miserable little thing. Got at least three times as many of those. My romneya are twice that size." Then, suddenly, she's stopped in her tracks. A ghastly pallor spreads across her face. "What...," she gasps, fighting for breath. *"What's that?"*

Disconcerted by her condition, you look to where she's pointing. "Hmm. I don't know. I think maybe it's an Allegheny vine," you say.

"You mean it's an *Adlumia fungosa?*"

"I'm not sure, but I think so."

"I don't have that." The words stick in her throat.

"No, I've never grown it either."

"I must have it!" There's a wild look in her eye. "I must have it!"

"Okay."

"I must have it now. Today!"

"All right."

"I won't sleep tonight if I can't find it!"

"I'm sure we can find one for you."

"I want more than one! I want dozens of them!"

Plants of all descriptions, along with birdbaths, sundials, statuary, urns, arbors, benches, fountains, pools, sculptures—the avaricious gardener sniffs them out, like a pig after truffles. And then trundles them back to the castle and hoards her treasures there, like Croesus his gold, oblivious to the fact that the bird of paradise alights only upon the hand that does not grasp. "What are you talking about? I've got a bird of paradise. *Strelitzia,* right? In fact, I've got fourteen of them. In the greenhouse. I counted them this morning."

The virtue contrary to Avarice is Generosity. And when it comes to gardening, we're hard-pressed to know whether the virtue isn't worse than the vice. The excessively generous gardener—like the chronic overtalker at dinner parties—is a creature to be both pitied and avoided. "Look," one of these menaces greets you on your back porch, "I've just dug up all this creeping Jenny and I couldn't bear to throw it out, so I thought of you right away, that it would be the perfect thing for that little damp spot at your place." You've told him a dozen times that you're attempting to develop a woodland garden using only native plants, and the last thing you need is invasive exotics overrunning everything. But you might as well talk to a fence post. "Oh, and I kept some of this lovely ground ivy for you, too." He produces a tray of the plant equivalent of avian flu. "And here's some of this spotted dead nettle. It's a tiny bit aggressive, so best to keep an eye on it." A tiny bit aggressive? The stuff makes Pol Pot look like the Dalai Lama.

But the generous-to-a-fault gardener isn't content with just handing over these terrorist specimens, so that you can pitch them into the first trash bin that comes to hand. He insists on helping you plant them. "No, no, the least I can do," he says. "I know how busy you are. I don't want to add to your workload, so let's just pop them in quickly and be done with it." Naturally, you have to go along with this, because you're trying your mightiest to practice the third contrary virtue, Kindness. This doesn't permit you to do what you want to do, which is to tell the generous gardener to take his unwanted plants and piss off. Instead,

you smile meekly while he plops his marauding monsters into your masterpiece. You know that by dinnertime they'll have engulfed your garden, at which point you'll abandon Kindness and give vent to the third deadly sin, Rage.

Before that can happen, though, the generous gardener is back with a massive box of vegetables. "I seem to have grown more than we need," he tells you, smiling amiably, as he passes over fourteen heads of wilted romaine lettuce and five cauliflower heads that have started to bolt. Year after year he grows more than he needs—hell, he grows more than half the city needs—but every year it's a big surprise. "Must be all that vegetable booster and 20-20-20 I socked onto them," he tells you, explaining how you're once again the beneficiary of his chemical largesse. You've tried repeatedly to direct him to the food bank, but he's undeterrable. Half an hour later he's back, lugging five-gallon buckets of plums. "Make a lovely jam," he tells you, as though you're going to eat jam at three meals a day for the rest of your life. And kiwifruit! I ask you: Why do these pathologically generous gardeners insist on producing hundreds of thousands of kiwis every year and expect you to deal with them?

What's most annoying about these overproducers is that their productivity draws an unwelcome comparison with your own situation. You're a helpless victim of the fifth deadly sin of gardening, namely, Sloth. Indolence. Laziness. Torpidity. The disinclination to action, exertion, or labor. You glance out the window. The lawn needs cutting and the edges trimming. Quackgrass has invaded the

mixed border and horsetail's spreading through the shrubbery. The hedges are starting to resemble Rastafarians.
The pots and planters desperately need watering. The
carrots are crying out to be thinned and the roses to be
sprayed. You're months behind on your staking and pruning and tying and training.

You survey the scene dispassionately, and you come to
a dreadful conclusion: you really don't give a shit. I mean,
how many years have you been working on this place? Year
after year, work, work, work. And where does it get you?
Nowhere. Next year you've got to work, work, work all over
again. Okay, so the first few years you could understand
it. You gladly made the necessary sacrifices in the service
of "The Garden." You had a vague, unspoken notion that
all of this labor, this blood and sweat, this wrenching of
backs and callusing of hands was an investment in some
unspecified future state of bliss, a state to be enjoyed forever once "The Garden" was completed.

You didn't cavil, you didn't complain, down there on
your knees in the mud. But as year followed year after
year, it began to dawn on you: you were doing the same
damn chores over and over and over again. The weeding, the watering, the shearing, the endless, mindless
maintenance. And now you realize with a startling flash
of insight: this work is not going to end. It's never going
to end. There isn't going to be any magical moment when
rough labor departs and indolence descends. This body-
bruising punishment isn't a necessary preparation for better days ahead, lazy days of wine and roses—no, it's a way

of life. Shocked to the core, you recognize the naked truth: these gardeners are a bunch of raving masochists. It's as though you've been enticed into some bizarre religious cult whose members get their jollies out of perpetual slave labor. Who in their right mind would want to be out there grubbing in the dirt and getting bitten by horseflies when they could just as easily be lying on the couch watching *Extreme Makeover*?

After your discovery, every molecule in your aching body urges you toward physical and mental inactivity. You don't want to battle the elements all summer trying to grow vegetables. You want to vegetate. You want to sprawl on a beach somewhere, bask in glorious sunshine. Go on, have a snooze, why don't you? a seductive voice whispers in your ear. You deserve it. The lawns can wait till tomorrow. Yes, I'll do it tomorrow. Mañana. Spread that warm tanning lotion on my back, why don't you? Ah...the torpid horticulturalist subsides into untroubled slumber.

Unfortunately for the slothful gardener, nineteen times out of twenty he has made the drastic miscalculation earlier in life of marrying, or at least becoming permanently entangled with, a person who practices the virtue contrary to sloth, Zeal—eager desire and active enthusiasm for something. Just as you're drifting away on the couch, your zealous companion bounds into the room, jaunty sun hat on her head, secateurs and trowel in hand, and exclaims, "What a gorgeous morning for gardening! Oh, do let's get out there, darling, before another minute's lost!" Gently, you attempt to explain that the middle of

January's too early in the year for gardening. "Oh, but we can do some planning!" she enthuses. Zealous gardeners are always planning something or other. "We could transplant the dogwoods to that corner over there. And have a mass of hydrangeas here. That would leave us more room to expand the rose bed out in this direction. What do you think, darling?"

It doesn't matter what you think—you're doomed. Zealous gardeners are forever expanding something somewhere, and it's always "we" who are going to do the expanding. "We" are going to be hauling in rocks as big as rhinoceroses and piling them up to create a waterfall. "We" are going to tear out the lawn and put in a Taj Mahal–scale reflecting pool. "We" are going to work in the garden right through the long weekend because it's so much *fun*. "Isn't this fun?" she beams as you're sprawled on the ground, locked in mortal hand-to-hand combat with a stubborn bigleaf maple root. "Aren't we the luckiest people in the world," she chimes, "to have all this time for gardening!"

Episodes like this are precisely why zealous gardeners and their slothful companions are so frequently described as gluttons for punishment. Which brings us to the sixth deadly sin of gardening: Gluttony. The vice of excessive eating and drinking. And here again the popular image of the gardener is absurdly mistaken. We're generally pictured as slender little persons who probably never eat at all. Or at most nibble at a bowl of fresh raspberries with a spoonful of fat-free yoghurt. Perhaps a cup of mint tea at the end of a long day.

The reality, as we know, is quite the opposite. No sooner have you gotten your wheelbarrow and spade out of the potting shed after a full breakfast than it's time to stop for a coffee and muffin. You agree to a second cup and another muffin while discussing whether to radically sheer back that willowleaf cotoneaster or cut it out altogether. By the time you've got your boots back on, found your gloves and sun hat, and trudged out to the barrow, it's time to pick a salad for lunch. The shelling peas are swelling their pods, so you have to pick a few and pop them into your mouth as you go. Then the ripe strawberries catch your eye, and you have to eat a few of those, too. You get the salad picked and get back to the house, where there's a lunch laid out that's big enough to stuff a soccer team. You eat voraciously on the grounds that you're working so hard in the garden you're burning a tremendous number of calories and need to keep your strength up. The same rationale authorizes your having a pint of stout with lunch.

After the meal you're stuffed so full you can hardly move, so you lie down on the chaise lounge to rest for a minute. The minute stretches into a long and delicious midafternoon digestive siesta, much like that of a lizard basking on sun-warmed stone. Afterward, you might wobble around in the yard for a minute or two, making vague passes at getting a few chores done, until it's time to stop for biscotti and hot chocolate. The resulting sugar rush propels you into a frenzy of activity whose results would be truly astounding if it weren't so quickly cut short by the siren song of the happy hour. After a few martinis on the patio, you've convinced yourself and everybody else that you've been working like a dog in the garden since dawn. Aperitif in hand, you stagger in to dinner. The dining room table's groaning under the weight of food, much of it great mounds of cauliflower, zucchini, and the like, donated by those excessively generous gardeners menacing the neighborhood. Wine flows freely. You finish up with an enormous bowl of plum and kiwi pudding and a couple of glasses of cognac. Stuffed to the eyeballs, you crawl on all fours to the bedroom and roll into bed like a huge, blubbery sea lion flopping on its rock. Just before passing out, you smile to yourself with satisfaction at your great accomplishments. Tomorrow will bring yet another arduous but rewarding day in the garden.

After several years of this excess, and maybe a couple of heart attacks, you're convinced by some crackpot self-help guru that you'd better dedicate yourself to the contrary virtue to Gluttony, which is Temperance. The avoidance of excess in eating and drinking. Light, wholesome, moderate meals. No snacking in between. No intoxicants whatsoever. A body fine-tuned by rational self-restraint. A mind sharpened by sobriety. What's astonishing in a regime like this is how much time gets freed for gardening. Endless hours open up between breakfast and lunch. The stretch from lunch to dinner seems an eternity. No wasted time at a happy hour. A simple meal of salad, rice, and tofu. The whole evening free to read Vita Sackville-West or practice ikebana. "The temperate life," as has been said, "has gentle pains and pleasures."

But let's be honest: after a few weeks of this regimen, life gets pretty damn boring. And that's where the seventh, and last, deadly sin slithers into the gardener's life. I speak, of course, of Lust. Yes, fleshly lust, libidinous sexual appetite. In certain gardening circles, it's considered good form to speak of carnal desire, if at all, only in a highly metaphorical sense. "I'm absolutely passionate about petunias." "Oh, how I lust for a *Styrax japonica!*" And all the rest. As though for us gardeners lust occurs only from the eyebrows up. As though carnal arousal is stimulated only by the body parts of plants.

As I've detailed elsewhere at considerable length, metaphorical meandering about one's passion for gardening serves only to mask a dreadful truth: that gardeners are a robustly lusty bunch. What penetrating speculations we might entertain as to why this is the case—maybe all the talk of germination and pollination and propagation; too many hours spent down there amidst the pistils and stamens and anthers. I usually delicately avoid mentioning the hanky-panky rife in horticultural organizations, but most garden clubs make Playboy clubs look like Presbyterian churches. The knowing smiles upon club members' faces at meetings, the mischievous twinkles in their eyes, the bouquets of flowers they clutch in their sweaty hands, like brides, as they sweep into rooms packed with hundreds of throbbing bodies. The howls of laughter, the gay swirl of skirts. Canny winks during the reading of the minutes about bedding plants and hot frames. Have you never wondered why, at the end of a garden club meeting, the half-dozen token males in attendance emerge beaming like nasturtiums? Not to mention the club coach trips, the overnight sojourns to distant garden shows and garden tours. Oh, sure! It makes you wonder if the day can be far away when once-respectable garden publications start running steamy personal ads. "Naughty alpine gardener seeks fun-loving companion for randy romps around the rockery. Size not an issue."

Against this current of concupiscence one must stand steadfast, alone if necessary, wrapped in the mantle of the contrary virtue to Lust: Chastity. Sweet chastity, the refraining from indecency and sexual excess. The pure of heart are not about to wander the garden muttering the prayer of Saint Augustine: "Oh Lord, give me chastity...but do not give it yet." No, you and I will cleave to dear chastity now, will we not? We'll abandon those garden club hotbeds and live as purely and virtuously as lilies, cultivators, as Edmund Spencer put it, of "the flower of faith and chastity."

It soothes my troubled heart to think of gardeners far and wide united in a renewed dedication to chasteness. And united too in all the other virtues: in humility rather than in pride; in love rather than in envy; in kindness rather than in anger; in generosity rather than in avarice; in zeal rather than in sloth; in temperance rather than in gluttony.

Now, you are with me in this, aren't you?

On the Isle of
Saints and Scholars

IF, AS HAS been said, mysticism lies at the heart of every great garden, where better to go garden touring than Ireland. It's a country I long wanted to visit, my ancestral homeland, but the nearest I'd previously come was at the age of ten, sailing out from Liverpool with my family to begin a new life in Canada and seeing the distant hills of Ireland disappearing into the North Atlantic mists. In a mad moment many years later, I signed on to lead a group of gardeners from various corners of Canada on a weeklong tour of Irish gardens.

No sooner had we arrived on the Emerald Isle than I felt intuitively I'd come home, though to a home I'd never known. Over the past quarter century no country in western Europe has evolved more dramatically, from a largely rural, impoverished, insular, and pious society to one that is urban, prosperous, globalized, and secular. The Celtic tiger does not feed on leprechauns and limericks. But still a mystic otherness clings to the place, at least in the imagination of romantic fools from Liverpool. I was, in short, as ripe for the plucking of Paddy-quackery as any stout-soaked Boston Irish traipsing to the Rose of Tralee Festival.

Eleven of us duly assembled in Dublin City. Any misgivings concerning the sausage-factory ambience of tour bus travel were allayed by the anticipation of experiencing fine gardens with a group of congenial fellow gardeners. For as we know, notwithstanding their eccentricities, gardeners are with rare exceptions the most pleasant of persons. Charged with enlivening the group experience, the tour host (myself, in this case) occupies an exalted, if somewhat precarious, position. Ideally, the host ought to be impressively credentialed, knowledgeable in most facets of horticulture, discreet, and charming. Failing this, the host may rely upon peculiarity of temperament seasoned with a great deal of good-natured bluster. This is the strategy I adopted as host of our Irish ramble.

But things got off to a shaky start. Endowed with a head of perhaps excessively long and excessively red hair, I had anticipated that in Ireland I should find myself commingling with a multitude of homegrown redheads and be immediately embraced as one of them. An initial stroll through old Dublin's manic traffic- and pedestrian-clogged streets put that illusion to flight. With seldom a redhead to be seen and every male a croppie boy with hair too short to justify owning a comb, I found myself being gawked at by respectable Dubliners and giggled at by urchins. The heads of passengers in passing tour buses would turn in unison to stare at me. At one point a rather brazen and slightly intoxicated American matron, mistaking me for a genuine Irishman, accosted me in a pub, threw her arms about me, declared that I was "a cute one," and faced me toward a battery of cameras wielded by her hooting companions. I think of myself immortalized as a true Irishman on the wall of some dreadful rumpus room in Cincinnati.

Our group of gardeners, it goes without saying, never stooped to antics of this sort. We gathered at Buswells Hotel, a converted eighteenth-century Georgian town house, to meet our local guide and establish our modus vivendi. Mere steps away was venerable Trinity College, founded by the first Queen Elizabeth and watched over by sentinel statues of the poet Oliver Goldsmith and the great orator Edmund Burke. Close by stood the National Library, whose reading room was featured in Joyce's *Ulysses*, and nearby Newman House, where the poet Gerard Manley Hopkins taught. At hand were smoky pubs where Joyce and Brendan Behan drank and the narrow alleys of Temple Bar, where the ghosts of Wilde and Yeats may wander. The district throbbed with the thrilling pulse of a literary history I'd known for years from books alone.

The assigned local guide is pivotal on expeditions of this sort. Where we might have been freighted with a pedant or a drone, we were instead blessed with a spirited Irish lady named Pat McColgan who, besides dispensing standard guiding information, regaled us throughout the week with tales of sexual, financial, and other indiscretions on the part of local politicians and fellow luminaries.

The first morning, after a "full Irish breakfast" of near-lethal cholesterol content, we clambered aboard an enormous tour bus expertly maneuvered through narrow, twisting streets by driver Dermot Geary, who added his own droll commentary to Pat's patter. Our first stop was the renowned city garden of Val and Helen Dillon. A gifted plant collector, author, television personality, and lecturer, honored by the Royal Horticultural Society, Helen's as sharp as a pruning knife and seldom caught short for want of an opinion on matters horticultural. Her walled city garden behind a stately Georgian home is divided into multiple compartments, the whole centered by a long, formal reflecting pool. It is a place of surpassing beauty, selected as one of "the 50 Best Gardens in Europe" by the *Independent* newspaper. Part of its genius lies in Helen's use of ordinary plants—large teasels and ornamental grasses, for example—in combination with rare and exotic species collected on expeditions overseas. The deployment of color, texture, and form to create smart compositions that harmonize into a coherent whole is exceptional. Dillons' is one of those gardens that makes you want to dash home, tear out everything you've done so far, and start all over again (after having first won the lottery).

That was the auspicious beginning to seven days of touring that ushered us into some of the most distinguished private gardens in the Greater Dublin area. We experienced a romantic Robinsonian garden, a perfect small, suburban garden packed with miniatures and exotics, and the grandeur of great estates. We toured walled gardens dating back to the eighteenth century, now being restored to their former glory, new gardens being created from meadows, and gardens tumbling beyond the control of their aging owners into an unkempt and melancholy beauty.

"I do not want what I haven't got," chirped Irish chanteuse Sinead O'Connor in her heyday, but you could hardly expect a gang of hard-rock Canadian gardeners tramping through all this magnificence to share the sentiment. Gardening is an acquisitive art, and there is much in the Irish landscape to provoke rank covetousness. Repeatedly, shamelessly, we were wanting things we did not have. Stone features, for example. The Irish possess an ancient genius for stonework—"the last of Europe's stone age race," British poet John Betjeman celebrated them as being—and the countryside is charmed with megalithic tombs, standing stones, ancient abbeys, and the crumbling remains of fantastic castles. And walls. Stone walls to exhilarate any gardener this side of the Niagara escarpment. Irish growers appear to set forth not in search of a home, nor even a garden, but of a walled space within which a garden might be planted. Restoration of old walled gardens has become something of a national obsession, with public funds poured into restoring historic gardens like Kylemore Abbey Victorian Walled Garden in County Galway, where six acres are completely walled in with brick and stone. At stately Powerscourt Estate, in the gently rolling Wicklow

Mountains south of Dublin, the walled garden encloses the largest herbaceous border in Ireland. But many smaller gardens, too, are surrounded by stone or brick walls upon which fruit trees are espaliered, climbing roses trained, or clematis, jasmine, tropaeolum, honeysuckle, and other climbers encouraged to drape. Structures of beauty in themselves, the walls create a marvelous sense of enclosure, buffer tender plants from wind, and provide microclimatic advantages. Some properties—such as lovely Bray Garden in County Wexford—are blessed with old stone outbuildings that provide both shelter and an achingly romantic hardscape.

Along coastal areas particularly, we were astonished at the rare and tender plants that flourish in the island's moist and mild Gulf Stream climate: tree ferns and cordyline palm trees, rhododendrons, eucryphia trees blooming with masses of white flowers, the cinnamon bark tree, the California poppy bush, the Chilean fire bush, passion vines, banana trees, watsonia from South Africa, and innumerable other species. But it's not just in sheltered gardens that exotics flourish. After our tour was concluded, Sandy and I went camping in the west country, and out on the wild Connemara coast saw swaths of Chilean gunnera growing like giant rhubarb in the ditches—farmers complaining, as farmers do, about what a pestiferous weed they are—naturalized montbretia running orange riot everywhere, and fuchsias flourishing like weeds, in places forming hedgerows sassy with scarlet bloom. (By way of a sobering note, certain climatologists are now speculating that increased melting of the polar ice cap due to global warming may result in cold arctic waters pushing the Gulf Stream farther south in the Atlantic, thus dooming Ireland to far more frigid conditions.)

As with stone, water was a feature of many of the gardens we visited. The large estates of the old Anglo-Irish ascendancy—like Powerscourt in County Wicklow, Castlewellan and the sublime Mount Stewart in County Down—invariably boast at least one lake amid naturalistic plantings of trees and shrubs, often with elaborate fountains. We also visited Mount Usher in County Wicklow, hailed as a nearly perfect example of the romantic paradise Robinsonian garden. Dating back over a century to the revolutionary ideas of Irish designer William Robinson, this twenty-acre garden contains more than four thousand species of trees, shrubs, and other plants from around the world, laid out along both banks of the gently cascading Vartry River.

Perhaps as a counterpoint to the wildness of weather and topography, we detected a mania for topiary: the clipping and shearing of box, beech, and holly hedges, yew trees sheared into fantastic shapes, geometrical beds outlined by heather hedges, and bay trees clipped into domes. We saw outstanding examples on the grand estates—Mount Stewart's eccentric Shamrock Garden features a high hedge of English yew from the top of which fantastic topiary figures rise, the whole enclosing a topiary yew tree trained to form an enormous Irish harp. But even along country lanes we came upon lovely, small gardens of meticulously sheared hedges, trees, and shrubs. While still on the picturesque Ards Peninsula in "the North" we were delighted by a private garden featuring dozens of clipped shrubs which from the roadway looked like the back of the heads of an assembled crowd—perhaps a congregation—all turned toward a looming central topiary, like the chancel of a verdant church, in front of which an outlandish *Bronze Boy with Fish* fountain spewed water from the fish's gaping mouth. Out in the middle of nowhere, surrounded by meadows and copses, there sat this ridiculous, magnificent salute to the ancient guild of topiarists.

Many of the smaller towns and villages we passed through were charming to the brink of cloying, in part due to an inflorescence of planters and pots in every corner and hanging baskets dangling from every pole. A government-sponsored initiative called the Tidy Towns Competition appears to help inspire this omnipresence of planters, many of them beautifully rendered. Over seven hundred communities participate in the annual competition, which has been running for more than half a century; the winner pockets a handsome cash reward and the title of Ireland's Tidiest Town. The undertaking raises disquieting questions about how susceptible gardeners can be to bribery. Occasionally we'd come across a town, such as Sligo or Tipperary, whose inhabitants were having nothing to do with Tidy niceties. The honest drabness of these working towns provided welcome relief. But elsewhere, pubs, police stations, and campgrounds were all fair game for proliferating planters. On the Beara Peninsula, we stayed in a tiny campground in the backyard of a genial little Irish-man named Mr. O'Shea. His entire garden and the walls of his whitewashed cottage were swathed in planters and bas-kets, many containing petunias that he spent most of his waking hours deadheading. He was justifiably proud that his efforts had been rewarded by his grounds having been named the Best Small Garden in Ireland.

Lushness is the matrix of the Irish garden, since the country experiences a steady supply of moisture through-out the year. Our visit, however, came in the dying days of "the wettest summer ever recorded," which had destroyed 80 percent of the apple crop and ruined much of the hay. In Connemara we saw hay spread across stone walls in a forlorn attempt at drying it; little haystacks had pathetic wee hankies spread on top to keep the relentless showers off. But the hydrangeas loved it—hydrangeas everywhere, magnificent moptops in outrageous pinks and blues. And the looming gray skies were counterbalanced by a brilliant, shimmering green. "There is some alchemy of climate in Ireland that bedews the countryside with an unmistakable personality," wrote Sean O'Faolain. "It is in the softness of color, the mobility of the light, the gentleness with which sound caresses the ear."

Another alchemy suffuses the countryside, too: some powerful amalgam of history, piety, lyricism, and longing that especially haunts old graveyards and ancient monas-tic ruins. We felt it profoundly at Slievemore Deserted Village on Achill Island in County Mayo, where dozens and dozens of crumbling stone "booley houses," temporary summer shelters used by farmworkers but abandoned en masse around the time of the Great Famine, spoke of the dramatic social collapse that occurred in remote rural Ireland. The Irish poet Oliver Goldsmith wrote in *The Deserted Village*:

> Sunk are thy bowers, in shapeless ruin all,
> And the long grass o'ertops the mouldering wall,
> And, trembling, shrinking from the spoiler's hand,
> Far, far away, thy children leave the land.

While in County Down, we wended our way up to the mist-covered Mountains of Mourne. This was the countryside my father knew as a boy, and I had made a point of bringing to Ireland a small vial of my parents' ashes. (My mother was Liverpool Irish but had never set foot in Ireland, nor ever voiced any desire to do so.) We parked the car at the foot of one of the higher hills and started up its sodden, grassy slopes. Still feeling the effects of knee surgery, Sandy opted to sit and rest partway up while I continued to climb. The mists lifted off before I reached the summit, revealing a landscape of softly rounded hills alive with grasses being combed and stroked by the warm wind. I took the vial of ashes from my bag and thought for a while about my parents. I thanked them for all they'd done for me and my brothers, forgave them for the things they'd done poorly, then cast the ashes to the wind. As I rejoined Sandy, a cry drew our attention upward. Two great, black ravens were flying toward the summit I'd just left. They separated and circled the peak from opposite sides three times, calling to one another in the mysterious tongue of ravens. Their circling complete, they reunited and flapped off toward Newry, where my father had lived. We stood astonished, not quite believing what we'd seen. When I recounted this episode later, a wise old Irish woman told me, "Oh, it's not surprising at all that you'd see ghosts up there."

Entranced by that first Irish tour—as new visitors to Ireland tend to be—Sandy and I repeated the exercise the following year. Once again in the capable hands of tour guide Pat and coach driver Dermot, our group first proceeded to the National Botanic Gardens, spread over fifty acres, in which grow more than twenty thousand plant species. Our guided tour focused on the spectacular greenhouses containing cacti, orchids, succulents, and numerous tropicals, including an astonishingly large and somewhat menacing Amazon water lily—proclaimed a modern wonder of the world when first introduced to Europe—and on the many choice tree specimens in the arboretum.

In the rapidly changing countryside of County Meath, north and west of Dublin City, we visited Butterstream Garden, which was described by *House and Garden* magazine as "the most imaginative garden in Ireland." (This is the sort of description guaranteed to raise the hackles of other imaginative gardeners.) We were greeted on the entrance lawn by Jim Reynolds, a robust character endowed with the Irish gift for storytelling laced with slyly self-deprecating humor. He led us through a succession of garden compartments—a spring garden, a stream garden, a green walk, a hot-colored garden, and an old rose garden—each framed inside a hedge of beech, thorn, or yew. This mansion of garden rooms began in the family's farm fields twenty-five years ago with Jim's "irrational urge to possess a few roses."

As we carried on through the white garden and herbaceous borders, Jim described how at the outset he naively assumed he could grow anything that took his fancy—"a few camellias, acacias, lots of rhododendrons, an embothrium or two. The possibilities seemed endless." But not for long; victims of hard winter frosts and incompatible heavy limestone clay soil, "the ungrateful plants persisted in dying." He eventually opted for "more sensible" installations, next showing us the obelisk garden—a square of ingeniously clipped box centered by a very tall and unmistakably phallic obelisk. The pool garden featured a small Tuscan temple reflected in a lily pool surrounded by pavement and formal lines of box and terra cotta pots. Farther on was a gorgeous small courtyard looking out on a pair of canals bordered with grass and lime allées.

Created single-handed, the garden had become, Jim confessed, something of a monster. Weeds from the surrounding farmlands were a persistent menace. Hedges and topiary cried out for incessant shearing. Repeatedly sprinkled by summer showers, lawns required regular cutting. The canals had become fouled with long drifts of filamentous algae. Jim shrugged and laughed, admitting that he finds creating new garden spaces far more satisfying than maintaining established ones. Sound familiar?

It was time to return to Val and Helen Dillon's brilliant walled garden in Dublin City. Despite a busy schedule, Helen accompanied us through the garden, discussing its design and identifying many of its uncommon specimens. Val took several of us into the heart of the garden—the composting area—where we enthusiastically compared notes on the aesthetic delights of shredding.

On our first visit, Sandy and I had been struck by Helen's use of the tall, airy grass *Stipa gigantea,* which she'd planted at regular intervals along the front of the vividly colored herbaceous borders that run down either side of the reflecting canal. Red and other hot colors predominate on one side, blues and other cools on the other. We'd scurried home and transplanted our own stipas from background to foreground, hoping for a similar effect. Returning to Helen's garden the second year, we were shocked to see she'd torn the grasses out. She explained that an eminent British plantsman, over for a visit, had proclaimed that the grasses were all wrong for the front of a border, because their yellow stems were leaching out the vibrant blues and reds. And he was right, she agreed, so out they'd come.

After four days we packed our bags and boarded the coach for the trip south to Cork City. A heat wave wreaking much havoc in continental Europe was pushing temperatures in Ireland well above average. During the trip we hit patches of sticky roadway where the asphalt was melting from the sun's heat. The good news for us was that we enjoyed clear, sunny days throughout the tour—almost a meteorological miracle for Ireland, which normally averages three inches of rain in August.

We stopped en route at the Rock of Cashel, one of Ireland's premier ecclesiastical ruins. A bit farther south, the haunting ruins of Bridgetown Abbey, nestled in a lovely rural valley where the Aubeg and Blackwater rivers conjoin, offered us another glimpse of medieval ecclesiastical Ireland, without the swarms of jabbering tourists. Next morning, we explored the nearby town of Cobh, with its historic harbor and hilltop cathedral, and then Fota House and Gardens on Fota Island. The garden and arboretum here are of international importance because of the range and diversity of plants, including many Southern Hemisphere exotics, that flourish in the garden's Gulf Stream microclimate. We were fortunate to be guided around the estate by head gardener David O'Regan, who set more than a couple of hearts throbbing among our group, combining as he did great horticultural expertise with a classic Irish handsomeness.

Another of the tour's highlights was a visit to Lakemount Gardens in the hills above Cork City, the creation of Brian Cross and acclaimed as "one of Ireland's foremost gardens." An accomplished painter and raconteur, Brian showed us around his masterpiece, chatting modestly and amiably but all the while alert for, and plucking out, any weed that dared show itself. Few did. There was, however, no shortage of wonderful old stone statuary and troughs that Brian had scooped up at estate sales. He also has a collection of larger-than-life pottery vases that he acquires from a potter friend and skillfully arranges amid ornamental grasses and foliage plants.

Our final day was taken up with a journey to the hills of County Kerry, where we visited Muckross House and Gardens near Killarney. The gem of 25,000-acre Killarney National Park, the Muckross estate is one of Ireland's most popular attractions. And with good reason. Completed in 1843, the house itself is splendid, containing a stunning collection of original antique furnishings, draperies, and artifacts, and situated on the impossibly picturesque shores of Muckross Lake. The 50 acres of garden are informal in layout, with expansive lawns and woodlands that blend perfectly into the surrounding vistas of lake and mountains softened by forests of oak, birch, and arbutus. It's a landscape justifiably hailed as one of the world's outstanding places of beauty.

As old Ireland hurtles into affluent modernity, her countryside lies vulnerable to urban sprawl, expanding freeways, and the excesses of Celtic Disneyland tourism. As elsewhere, the work of gardeners provides a counterbalance to the forces of uglification. The gardens we visited were testament to the enduring appeal of harmonious places and to the genius of gardeners in helping to preserve the lyrical and mystical elements of their native landscape.

Passionate Plantings

NOT LONG AGO I turned my attention to writing a novel—an undertaking that consumes one's focus as relentlessly as the most feverish days in the garden—and saw it duly published with the title *Flame of Separation*. Setting modesty aside for a moment, I can tell you that this was a work of penetrating psychological insight and profound metaphysical speculation. Prior to its publication by an esteemed but penurious small press, I had pitched the story to a once-reputable Toronto publishing house and received in reply a brief letter advising me that "we never publish books involving paranormal phenomena, but we'd be delighted if you would consider writing for us a funny book about dogs." (Needless to say, I'm hard at work on that very project at the moment.) Following its publication, my paranormal novel was greeted with a glowing review in one newspaper, which included the heartening comment that "although Kennedy has been a fixture on the British Columbia writing scene for more than a decade, nothing in his previous writing has hinted at the power and grace he exhibits here."

Many hazards beset the poor but honest writer, scribbling long into the night in a gloomy room in the seediest imaginable neighborhood, unrecognized by an uncaring public and preyed upon by book reviewers, literary critics, publishers, editors, sales and marketing bean counters, literary agents, publicists, academic nitpickers, and assorted party animals. It is an impossible, preposterous way of life, a form of masochism so deviant that we must wonder why any individual chooses to pursue it.

But spare your tears, I beseech you, for the downtrodden wordsmith. The indignities of the publishing industry are as nothing, mere froth and effervescence, compared with the hazards of the gardening life and the pit of depravity into which that life can plunge its victims. That sounds extreme, I know. In a world racked with natural disaster, premeditated terror, and random violence, the notion of any significant imperilment inherent in horticulture seems a facile conceit. We are, after all, beguiled into imagining that the gardening life is an innocent walk through marvelous pleasure grounds, a stroll through attractive surroundings in which refined persons are engaged in sketching, reading, and reflective contemplation. Little children gambol on the lawn, and miniature dogs skip merrily at leash. All is serene and tasteful, everything in good order. There is nothing to unduly excite, nothing to confound, nothing to dismay. Gardening literature through the ages is rife with this sort of fiction: Old Francis Bacon writing that gardening is "the purest of humane pleasures." Or John Evelyn writing in the 1600s that "gardening is a labor full of tranquility and satisfaction; natural and instructive, and as such contributes to the most serious contemplation, experience, health, and longevity."

However, how many gardeners do you know who spend even a fraction of their days reclining on the grass, reading lyric poetry, or sketching fetching blooms? They're far more apt to be tortured by the agonies of garden design, the mental contortions of trying to get the color schemes right. Where's the contemplative purity in a bank of shrieking magenta pigsqueaks alongside drifts of malarial yellow tulips? None of those mythic idlers in the garden seem to throw their backs out heaving monstrous boulders around; none of them get poked in the eye by spiteful sticks or roughed up by sociopathic shrubs. They seem not to have their hearts regularly broken by winterkill or damping-off. Hurricane-force winds never flatten their delphiniums. They appear to suffer no infestations of blight, rust, scabs, or mottles. Malignant tent caterpillars don't tear their apple trees to pieces. A Garden of Earthly Delights, my dear? Are you putting me on? Gardening's more like a perpetual dash to the emergency ward.

The lyrical vision of the gardening life exposes what Thomas Carlyle called "that rosepink vapor of Sentimentalism." To view the garden through rose-colored glasses betrays a prudish passionlessness. Whereas we real-life gardeners are entirely the opposite. We are aficionados of catastrophe, the willing slaves of a divine madness. Above all else, we are tempestuously ardent in both our triumphs and our disasters. We may weep, we may exult, we may lament with the romantic, "Alas, the Rosaries, how they are broken down!" But we are never, ever passionless.

And here the pitfall lies for each of us. In venturing beyond the sensible environs of the picture postcard garden, the decorous path of massed coleus and marigolds, we too-ardent gardeners may enter forbidden precincts. The gardening life—which we undertook with such purity of purpose, such clarity of intent, such wholesomeness of outlook—gradually seduces us into the floricultural equivalent of desperate lust and unbridled raunchiness.

Not long ago I attended a meeting of a certain garden club and was shocked at how, all through the evening, talk was running hot about extending the life of cut flowers by doctoring their water with Viagra pills. I'm reminded of a news story about a sixty-two-year-old man in Pennsylvania, Stitzer by name, who took to gardening in the nude as a protest against his neighbor's floodlights. Local residents said Mr. Stitzer had already become something of a regional curiosity by mowing his backyard while clad only in shoes and a thong. But then, one fateful day, he went out to weed the garden without even his thong on. Mr. Stitzer was convicted of gross indecency and—who knows?—may be languishing to this day in some squalid cell at Guantanamo Bay. His is a cautionary tale. We observe our gardening associates, we consider ourselves in the mirror and wonder: are we condemned, each of us, to end our days gardening au naturel in passionate defense of place?

The fall from grace begins innocently, like a childhood crush on some attractive classmate. Those exhilarating stirrings of something you've never felt before. Perhaps you've just acquired your first house—a "starter," as they say in the real estate ads—with a long-neglected garden, or a patch of scraggly lawn. Maybe it's only a tiny patio garden behind a rented town house. No matter; there's a stirring in the loins. Just as you couldn't take your eyes off that cutie three desks over in grade 6, you find yourself fixated on the possibilities of this ratty little patch of ground. You take to daydreaming, fantasizing about how things might unfold. You lie awake at night, unable to sleep from excitement and the juices of newly activated glands coursing through your warm blood.

A terrible shyness holds you back. Are you good enough, appealing enough to take this terrifying plunge? What if you fail? What if you're rejected or proved inadequate? You don't want to humiliate yourself, become a laughingstock. The palms of your hands are sweaty, your muscles as tight as stretched elastic bands. You're so nervous, you could die. And yet you must take the leap; you have no choice. Your attraction is an impetuous horse you're riding, and you are powerless to check its headlong rush.

Yes, it was like starting a love affair, wasn't it, that first mad foray into the garden? Those intoxicating days of stealing a kiss from a tender petal now and then. Charmed days, long before you'd ever heard of crown canker. The carefree bliss of life before botrytis blight. The unalloyed joy of believing that perennials were plants that lived forever. Like lovers in springtime, we planted with abandon, heedless of the future. And, oh! Remember the charm of those first dear plants, virginal as snowdrops in early spring: maidenhair fern and none-so-pretty, virgin's bower, and the chaste tree. Was ever there a more lovely charmer than our first Pink Cloud beauty bush? And the sublime innocence of those early roses: Dainty Bess and deep-lavender Angel Face, Fair Bianca and Little White Pet, The Fairy, Maiden's Blush, and Lavender Lassie. Fair-maids-of-France and fair-maids-of-Kent. Oh, break my heart, blue-eyed Mary, virgin's palm, and touch-me-not. Beauties all, comely and so pure.

This was enough. Surely this was more than enough. If only we might have frozen that moment in time, remained forever as we were: decorous and ingenuous, but ecstatic in the clarity of those first joyful plantings.

But was holy Chastity sufficient for us? No, alas, 'twas not. For the unruly pulse of lust began to beat within our bosoms. Deny it if you will, but here was the first insidious slithering in, like the serpent into Eden, of the enchantment that would prove to be our undoing. All but the most steadfast among us abandoned that initial angelic vision, giving way to crazy impulses, temporary conquests. We started growing impatiens. We wanted to sow our wild oats, to experience the world, to discover our true selves. The most impetuous of us became power gardeners, forever panting and forever young. We threw out the old and brought in the hottest new things. Passion flowers and blood flowers sprang up in our plantings. Burning bushes and the flame flower tropaeolum, along with Dancing Doll orchids. We sniffed the floribunda rose Sheila's Perfume. We took to growing Cupid's dart and the date palm. We started carrying a torch lily. Like moths to a flame we were bewitched by the Venus fly trap. We danced a fiery dance with flaming Katy. We were intoxicated, delirious. Feverfew sprang up everywhere. We planted the hybrid tea climber Cupid, soft rose-pink Debutante, and the large-flowered climber Dreamgirl. The most brazen of us pulled down our Dutchman's-breeches to reveal our gardener's garters. We planted the mattress vine and caroused on silken sheets beneath silk trees and silky wisteria, with only the scantiest of underthings covering our candytuft and Silver Mound artemisias. Oh, youth!

Still, all was not yet lost, because from these youthful mad pursuits, we fell truly in love with the gardening life. Recognizing that it was time to settle down and get serious, we began thinking in terms of lifelong commitment. Passion fused with romance, and we were moved to a proposal of marriage. Then it became a Cinderella thing, the diamond engagement ring and storybook wedding. We developed a fondness for pink lady's slippers and eau de cologne mint, the lipstick plant and powder-puff cactus.

Sweetheart ivy and bridal wreath spirea, spilling like a frothy white bridal dress. We planted the alba Belle Amour beside the hybrid rambler Wedding Day and double-white Winchester Cathedral. We proclaimed solemn vows to live happily ever after, as permanent as sempervivum and pearly everlasting. A blissful sentimentality suffused the gardens. Moonflowers and moonshine yarrow. Beguiling patches of love-in-a-mist, yellow floating heart and forget-me-not, the sensitive fern and the sensitive plant. We put in the modern climber High Hopes and the richly violet hybrid musk Wine and Roses. We talked emotionally of maybe planting baby's breath and baby blue eyes and the glory vine called baby's fingers. Entrancement indeed, this honeymoon stage of the gardening life. If only one might linger there a while, linger there forever.

But a gardening honeymoon lasts about as long as your average Hollywood marriage. As sudden as the overnight fall of golden ginkgo leaves in autumn, the bloom is off the rose. Your vow to stick with it "in sickness and in health" curdles into a cruel hoax as every plant pathology known to science comes stampeding into your garden. In place of rapture, you're suffering endless eruptions of root rot. How were you to have known that "in good times and in bad" entailed a lifetime sentence of fighting with quackgrass? The garden became a tangled mess of climbing bittersweet and Angel's Tears narcissus, huge, outlaw patches of busy Lizzie and black-eyed Susan. *O tempora! O mores!* The steps have been taken onto a perilously slippery slope.

And here I speak from the somber classroom of my own experience. Yes, I confess it, as I hope to confess it someday to Oprah, or perhaps to Dr. Joy Brown: I became a promiscuous gardener. Tantalized by the anorexic goddesses of the fashion magazines, I took to planting slender deutzia, slim-leaf tulip and slender lady palm. The lady fern came next, then dancing lady, wearing only the senecio called string of beads. I put in the floribunda China Doll and splashy cream and red Birthday Girl. Despite the best intentions, I found myself repeatedly distracted by passing beauties. Like many a gardener before me, I was seduced by the charm of floral novelty. But I give you fair warning: these enticements can bring ruination.

Things might start with a harmless little flirtation with sweet cicely. Then a dalliance with a very attractive February daphne. Perhaps a brief amor with a beguiling Russian olive. Next a charming encounter with a common myrtle. You can't resist the brilliant orange-red of Dolly Parton, the trembling yellows of Teasing Georgia, or the creamy apricot of miniature Party Girl. You convince yourself that it's only a phase. That you'll surely grow out of it and settle down. But soon there's a brooding Dalmation iris at the doorstep, and after her, a sloe-eyed Turkish hazel. Then an altogether too robust Swedish ivy. And a ravishingly scented Chilean jasmine. Disconcertingly, you discover creeping Jenny slinking around the place, and, even more alarmingly, a false heather whose intentions you know you can't trust. You wonder if colleagues can detect the alluring perfume of wild violet on your clothes.

By the time a stinking iris and a voodoo lily have joined the party, alarm bells are sounding, and you decide to put your foot down. But too late. Bog rosemary and swamp lily are already over in a damp corner, drinking too much and gossiping with two notorious lushes, the hybrid teas Brandy and Whisky Mac. Rising up in the middle of things, a certain ruby horse chestnut gives every indication of having had enhancement surgery. Soon the garden looks as if it is turning into a ruby fruit jungle, with the noisy arrival of hedgehog holly, corkscrew hazel, dogtooth violet, and dwarf bearded iris.

This is shameful philandering; who could deny it? The garden has become a riot of ravishment, voluptuaries and enchantresses cavorting wantonly among the mixed borders. Can any garden withstand such excesses, any more than a marriage can? Night after night the gardener flops into bed with the same sad refrain: Sorry, darling, not tonight, I'm all done in from root pruning.

An understandable bitterness rises like bile, and soon the garden is given over to problematic plantings of Dragon's Blood sedum, the chenopodium called fat hen, and the lamium henbit, mother-in-law's-tongue, and welcome-home-husband-though-ever-so-drunk. You consider going to counseling, to see if the relationship can be salvaged, but put it off until the deadheading's finished. Weeping willows and birches and weeping beeches predominate now. You sit forlornly for hours in a patch of Job's tears, sniffling under the handkerchief tree. Bleeding hearts drip mistily alongside love-lies-bleeding. All seems lost.

Finally the day dawns on which you're forced to admit to irreconcilable differences among the evergreen azaleas. There's no mistaking it: this relationship is at an end. You want your freedom, the chance to start over again someplace else. You're one in spirit with maudlin old Alfred, Lord Tennyson:

> Tears, idle tears, I know not what they mean,
> Tears from the depth of some divine despair
> Rise in the heart, and gather to the eyes,
> In looking on the happy Autumn fields,
> And thinking of the days that are no more.

Then, one morning, the pain of separation abated somewhat, you find yourself staring up into the brilliant red bloom of the climber Sublimely Single. With innocence long since gone and fidelity now fled too, dark, carnal appetites begin to throb, and the garden is soon overrun with panting concupiscence. Free of commitment, you run wild in a phase of horticultural mania. (And here I must speak from the perspective of the male gardener gone to pot.) Out go all the weeping this and bleeding that, replaced by raunchy bachelor buttons and a far-too-cocky bed of cockscomb. Prurient patches of bedstraw under a wayfaring tree. Staghorn ferns and staghorn Sumac bugling like young bucks in rut at a stag party. The dark-red climber Don Juan scrambling up to the compact shrub Boudoir. Lascivious old goat's beard leering at plants half his age. Recklessly, you plant feature specimens of wild Irishman near beds of philandering cuckoo flower. Then, in a paroxysm of horti-naughtiness, you introduce Naked Lady amaryllis and—with a tip of trowel to old Hugh Hef himself—bunny ears. You surround them with plantings of slobbering great hound's tongue and hairy lip fern. Like the hapless Mr. Stitzer, you take to gardening wearing only a thong.

Delirious, panting with lasciviousness, the male of the species becomes obsessed with the grand act of *ejaculatio*. You spend hours among the tumescences of hyacinths. You are now fixated on lithosperma and potentilla. Mandrakes are self-seeding everywhere. Your gay associates insist on loading you up with fairy wands and wild pansy. Somebody crosses the line by giving you the bushy floribunda Sexy Rexy. And, even worse, the daylily Crotchless Panties. You take to calling a certain body part Johnny-jump-up or, sometimes, sweet william. Your mixed border stands erect with red hot pokers and black snakeroot. Oh, the engorged glory of goldenrod, lancewood, and sweet rocket! For the masculine gardener, of course, size is everything. So you marvel at your Zulu giant, at your astonishing *Cardiocrinum giganteum*. At the size and thickness of your striped giant reed and your enormous wonga wonga vine. And of course, for when the climactic moment arrives, you've got balloon flowers and a rubber plant close at hand right beside your squirting cucumber.

But enough already with pathetic phallic fallacies, for lo! on the distaff side of the estate, deep within the garden, lies a secret bower suitable for Aphrodite herself. A place of sacred intimacies, bordered in privet and sweet box. You

enter a glorious rosary with the creamy white floribunda
French Lace and the flesh-pink rambler Lady Godiva.
Then, closer still, Cuisse de Nymphe, the Thigh of the
Nymph. And near the garden's very center—be still, my
beating heart!—underplanted with tufted hair grass, lies
a grove of pussy willows and pussy ears. Finally, beyond
tempting beds of labiate and convolvulus—oh, bless me,
father, for I have sinned!—a flowering cherry with honey
bush and sunburst honey locust.

You're lost. Besotted. Entirely unbalanced. Recklessly,
you begin experimenting with opium poppies and mes-
cal beans, eulalia grass, and the stone plant. Thus down
the slippery slope you continue. Depravity, debasement,
outright perversion begin working their sinister way into
your plantings. First, perhaps, a disturbing hint of voyeur-
ism with the introduction of Peeping Tom narcissus. What
else but an unfortunate fetish could explain the number
of lady's slippers you've got planted alongside your variegated cocksfoot? Perhaps you find yourself alone at night
in a dark corner of the garden spanking the monkey puz-
zle tree. Intimations of masochism underlie beds of Spar-
tan tulip and the obedient plant. A golden chain laburnum
hints of bondage. And overtones of sadism are unmistakable with the introduction of lace cactus and strap cactus.
The fingerprints of the Marquis de Sade himself are all
over your choice of the menacing yuccas Spanish bayonet
and Spanish dagger. You bring in a piggyback plant, a contorted willow, and an extremely twisted corkscrew rush.

Then, in a final, humiliating act of self-degradation, you find yourself lying under a Golden Showers rose in a bed of Lord Anson's blue pea.

You have hit the bottom of the slope. A burned-out horticultural case. Ruinous appetites have wrecked your body, left your spirit derelict and peccant. You find yourself mournfully tending an old man's cactus and a bald cypress, fumblingly trying to determine how much water you can pour onto a white bladder flower without getting drops on the floor. Quaking grass and hoary plantain have overrun the yard. You're repeatedly embarrassed by untimely exhalations from your gas plant. Though you can't speak of it from guilt and shame, your beds now seem mostly given over to the drooping star-of-Bethlehem and prostrate speedwell, with a pathetic scattering of limp angel's fishing rods and a flaccid *Diplopappus fruticosus*. Verticillium wilt is prevalent. For a while you take a lackluster interest in hanging baskets, but the whole drooping place reminds one of the Hanging Gardens of Babylon. Instead of *vera copula*, real intercourse, you're left with a bedraggled specimen of the interrupted fern and, most humiliatingly for the male, the shrimp plant. Not to mention the Mickey Mouse plant or the half-inch mint. You spend most of your time hiding behind the headache tree. You make a last, desperate bid to regain masculine vigor by manic fertilizing of your resurrection plant, asking yourself, Where's that nearby garden club's Viagra now, when you need it most?

But no. No. 'Tis over. The brilliant innocence of the chaste tree gone forever. The young, blood-red love of the passionflower fled. The fairy-tale honeymoon of bridal wreath spirea scarce remembered. The abiding bliss of love-in-a-mist evaporated. The naughtiness of flirting with Lady Godiva and voodoo lily never to be repeated. The seductiveness of pussy willows withered. The titillations of Peeping Tom narcissus no more. Not even the bittersweet heartache of parting with love-lies-bleeding.

Where can the deflated gardener possibly go in such desolation of spirit? To whom can one turn with passion thus spent and lust thus lost? The answer, of course, is right before your eyes. There's absolutely no need for lasting defeat or despair. After you've bottomed out completely, wandered disconsolate through the dark night of the horticultural soul, do what so many stricken victims have done before you, what I myself have done to wonderful effect: simply drop the gardening thing for a while. Take up something else, something altogether different. Like playing poker on the Internet, for example. Or maybe try your hand at writing. Why not write a funny book about dogs? Schmooze with approving publishers and amusing reviewers.

Then, once you've come to your senses, get back into the garden straightaway. Back into intimate Aphrodite's Arbor and mischievous Cupid's Bower. Cozy up with What A Peach, cavort with a sport of Garden Party. Vamp all night with All That Jazz. Yes, for sweet intoxication's sake, get back into the garden, back to the tumult and madness, and feel the passion anew, darlings. Yes, feel the passion anew.

Construction Workers

"GOOD FENCES MAKE good neighbors," the poet Robert Frost observed. Gardeners, of course, know all about fences and fence lines, and perhaps more than they should about their neighbors as well. But fences can be difficult, and the possession of a "good" fence is rather like the living of a good life—easier in principle than in practice.

There is, to begin with, as the poet reminded us, a need to address what we are fencing in or out and whom this is likely to offend. My own objectives have been simple enough: our fences are designed and constructed for two practical purposes. The first is to exclude herds of deer intent upon demolishing our plantings. The second is to contain the gardens inside an almost-manageable space, to prevent them from spilling out all over the acreage and hastening our departure to the madhouse.

Our fences have not entirely succeeded in either objective. Deer, as many gardeners know to their sorrow, possess magical powers that enable them to penetrate any fence they choose. They may leap over, they may wiggle through tiny apertures, they may simply await a gate left carelessly open—but they'll be in, sooner or later. Still, our fences have proved provisionally successful at minimizing their intrusions, although entirely ineffectual at keeping the gardens contained. You know how it is: never enough space in the garden for all the plants on hand, never enough colleagues on whom to unload surplus plants. So you start creating new planting areas beyond the fences, succumbing to delusions that these are "deer-proof plants" and won't require any extra work. Eventually the whole estate becomes littered with outpost plantings, most of them obscured behind makeshift fences erected after deer have munched down the deer-proof plants.

But I'm not convinced that these rural fencing follies are anywhere near so tortuous as the dilemmas facing urban fencers. Certainly, the question of a fence giving offense is far more germane. Suppose you've got a chapter of Hells Angels living next door. You're prepared to tolerate the roar of Harleys and the blood-curdling screams from all-night partying, but you draw the line at having empty beer cans tossed into your bergenias. Nevertheless, how high and how stout a fence can you erect without offending the lads' sensibilities and causing bad feelings? In more traditional neighborhoods, the ancient rite of chatting over the backyard fence may still be practiced. A high barricade erected in such a milieu is sure to create an aura of exclusivity that will not soon be forgotten or forgiven. As well, those seeking seclusion must reckon with the quirk of human nature that needs to see what's happening on the other side of any fence. You'd almost have to provide viewing slots, as is done at construction sites, to accommodate the legitimate curiosity of passersby.

Plus, there's the question of fence design. Do you prefer a prim little picket, or a proper sort of paling, or a full-blown palisade? Chain-link fencing strung from steel posts set in concrete makes for a durable fence but falls a few links short of aesthetically satisfying. You'll see certain gardeners, stuck with such fences for whatever reason, transforming them into living tapestries by interweaving vines through the lifeless wire. Indeed, the decoration of indecorous fences with flowering vines, espaliered trees, fan-trained roses, and other splendors is one of the great contributions gardeners make in the realm of fencing.

I myself am partial to the traditional split-rail fence, and I have split many hundreds of rails from downed western red cedar logs on the property. Robust with rustic charm, this fencing style has the added advantage that the fence can be collapsed and rebuilt elsewhere if one is looking for something to do. On the downside, its portability leaves it exposed to pilferers, and a number of serviceable split-rail fences have mysteriously gone missing on the island over the years. Also on the downside, cedar posts, sunk into the earth decades ago for gateposts, arbors, and bowers, do tend to rot out and begin leaning deviantly. It's disconcerting, this rotting away of fences and other structures you vividly remember building not all that long ago. Such was the case with our fence-cum-rose arbor. I suspect there may be a universal principle concerning rose arbors, to the effect that once all climbing and rambling roses have achieved their desired size and magnificence, the arbor upon which they're climbing will need to be replaced.

The prospect can be especially disheartening when the arbor in question is as cunningly wrought as ours was, achieving the elevation of roses, golden hops, and clematis while fencing out deer and other miscreants, but in a way that maintained a vista of lawns and woodlands beyond. Using choice pieces of ancient cedar split-rail fencing, we had set eight-foot posts in gravel capped with concrete at ten-foot intervals. Each post was topped with a crosspiece and knee brace, and the row of crosspieces was connected on top by three thin, horizontal cedar rails. Galvanized stucco wire strung between the posts kept the deer out but preserved a sense of openness. At either end of the fence, a square bower of similar construction provided a covered entranceway. Already colonized by mosses and lichens, the cedar pieces had given an instant feeling of antiquity to our fledgling garden, recalling Milton's "Yon flourie Arbors, yonder Allies green." By any standard the structure was an aesthetic and practical masterpiece, whose merits I didn't hesitate to trumpet in print and conversation.

Twenty years later, with the roses at their heaviest, the arbor began listing tipsily. A few stout braces wedged into the breach only postponed an inevitable collapse. Tottering and frail, the arbor had lost the aura of excellence it previously enjoyed. It was really too squat, for one thing, oppressively low-slung. Where once it had loomed over our first small plantings, it now seemed to cower beneath maturing trees and vines. Its previously sturdy structural members seemed shrunken to little more than sticks, as thin and brittle as birds' bones. No question about it, we were insufficiently embowered. The time had arrived for arbor replacement.

It's an amazing thing that with certain gardeners—generally, but not exclusively, males of the species—reserves of energy well up like gushing oil when a new construction project hoves into view. If chain saws, mauls, or other signifiers of machismo are involved, even the most lethargic couch potato will set to enthusiastically lacing up steel-toed boots and pulling on no-nonsense leather gloves. This was precisely my disposition when a decision was made to proceed with a new arbor.

New and improved, I hasten to add. The structure would be taller, for starters, more copasetic with the stature of the garden. Its members would be heftier. Most critical of all, the arbor would be permanent; sixty years of age, I had developed the firm conviction that any new projects—be it this arbor, or the new roof, or the new pump house—must be executed in a way that would outlast me. No more "good enough for now" gimcrack projects. I don't want to be redoing those in my eighties. We would do it right this time, and it would suffice.

Step 1 was to locate a worthy red cedar log from which at least the posts could be split. All cedar scores high in rot resistance, due to a chemical in the wood called thujaplicin, but there's a considerable gradient between tight-grained old growth and wide-grained second growth. Thirty years ago I might have contentedly banged my way through an adolescent log that was all sapwood, wide growth rings and large knots, but no longer. I wanted a tree that had grown in crowded conditions, slow and straight out of dry, stony ground. For some time I'd had my eye on a large cedar that had blown down near the back property line, after that pathological clear-cut on the adjacent acreage had exposed our trees to winter storms.

On a hot summer afternoon I entered the cool forest, hacked my way through a tangle of windfall branches, and set my chain saw into the tree's trunk near its fluted base. This is a juncture at which any number of things can happen, almost all of them bad. Suspended horizontally by its upturned roots at one end and its branches at the other, the tree can suddenly pinch the bar of your saw, locking it into the wood like the mythic sword in stone. The trunk might split down its length from the sudden release of tensions created by its positioning. Or, with the cut complete, the log may fly sideways a lethal "sweeper" knocking you ass-over-teakettle. Nothing of the sort occurred, however. Severed cleanly, the trunk slumped to the ground. The bole was perfectly sound, no heart rot at the center, its growth rings so densely packed together you couldn't tell one from the next. I calculated the tree to be at least 150 years old. The grain ran perfectly straight up the bole. This was a log sent by the gods.

I bucked the trunk into ten-foot lengths, about three feet in diameter, and peeled off the bark. With sledge-hammer and steel splitting wedges I cracked each log in half, then split each half into three rails. Oh, the glory of that work—the sweating and panting of it, the brawny arc of the swung sledge, the John Henry ring of steel driving steel, the resigned sigh of the bole as it at last succumbed to splitting. And what rails emerged—straight and stout, smooth as young flesh on their outer skin, grainy down their split sides. Because the tree was still green and heavy with sap, I couldn't carry the largest rails but had to flip them end-over-end like an enfeebled Scot failing to toss his caber. All of this was prodigiously muscular stuff, speaking to one's inner Hercules in a way that deadheading the roses never can. I left the rails scattered on the forest floor to dry out over the summer, first returning to them with ax and adze to chip away the sapwood from the portion of each post that would be buried in the ground, so as to further delay rotting. I imagined myself connected, in spirit if not in skill, with generations of cedar carvers who had done precisely the same thing all up and down the coast.

In the bracing days of autumn we hauled the rails, now considerably lighter, out of the bush. The old arbor came down with the grace of an aged ballet dancer. Some of its better pieces we retained for minor roles in the new struc-

ture. The new poles were erected with a fitting solemnity.
We packed small stones around their bases underground
to deter rotting and probably should have scorched the
butt ends of the poles for longer life, as the coastal peoples
did, but we didn't.

The new arbor stands now like the columns of an
acropolis. The enlarged gateway bowers are grand enough
for the Queen of Sheba to enter through. The roses and
clematis, cut back to accommodate construction, are free
now to climb to dizzying heights. All is as it should be, we
told ourselves, recalling Milton's "bowre of earthly bliss,"
because that's a job we'll never have to do again. Having
said it, some part of me wanted to weep because it's true.

Which was all the more reason to get busy on something else, like constructing a new garden vantage point,
for instance. The accumulation of vantage points is a
fetish with certain gardeners, and for those thus afflicted
no toil is too arduous, no weather too inclement for the
work involved. Our new undertaking would entail hauling,
rolling, and dragging enormous stones uphill to create an
elevated prominence from whose heights we might survey the sweep of gardens, lawns, and woodlands. Sort of a
budget-priced Capability Brown landscape job.

Even before completion, the project reeked of redun-
dancy. The garden already boasted several vantage points.
A high, wooden deck attached to the summerhouse
provides views of the garden and house on one hand and
lawns and woodland on the other. Farther along the hillside, another wooden deck looks down from a slightly

different angle. At the remote northern end of the garden, a small path leads beneath yet another rose arbor and up rustic steps to a wooden bench nestled amid the roots of an enormous western red cedar. For looking upward rather than down, we have a wooden bench under the refurbished rose bower that provides views across the garden and up the hillside. Last, a patio alongside the house gives intimate views of a pool and cascade and the lower portion of the garden. Any reasonable individual would conclude that these options are more than sufficient. But construction-work gardeners are seldom reasonable and, too long denied a challenging project, they become restless, like hibernating bears with insomnia. We want to be out and about, doing something, and for the vantage point fetishist, few projects call more seductively than the creation of a new lookout.

This enterprise was conceived in summer, as we debated what to do with a pile of surplus stone. Stones by their nature are content to lie about, but gardeners prefer that stones, like everything else, be given a purpose in life. There is for us, as for Ecclesiastes and innumerable folksingers thereafter, "a time to cast away stones, a time to gather stones together." This was a time for gathering. Inspired by our Irish adventures, we first concocted a wild scheme to create a Gothic archway of lichen-crusted stone evocative of crumbling abbey ruins. Mercifully this delusion was done away with long before it could be attempted, though we abandoned the scheme less from recognition of its intrinsic folly than from my certainty that I could never get a free-standing stone archway to stay up. But the stones remained, as stones do, and eventually we struck upon the notion of a stony vantage point atop the hill. We imagined ourselves at the height of summer, reclining at our ease on this new prominence, the tumultuous beauty of the garden beneath us experienced as never before.

To justify the time and hard labor involved, it was first necessary to catalogue the inadequacies of the existing vantage points. The view from the summerhouse deck, we agreed, was badly obscured by the robust growth of a nearby *Acer griseum*. The second wooden deck, besides falling apart from age, provided a less-than-flattering view of the house. The secret bench beneath the cedar tree lacked a true vista and was home to hordes of mosquitoes. Looking uphill from the bench within the flowery bower was disagreeable in the afternoon, because of sunshine right in your eyeline. The patio alone passed muster, chiefly because it houses two knockoff Edwardian steamer chairs, and after a hard day in the trenches few things satisfy more fully than putting one's feet up and reclining comfortably beside the pool. Too comfortably, in fact. The patio's seductive pleasures are the primary reason the other vantage points are underutilized. We convinced ourselves that by creating an elevated rampart, a position from which garden and house might be seen at a more flattering angle, we would surely be lured from our lazy repose down below.

And so we set to work. The design called for a surrounding rock wall about five feet high, its center packed
with fill and a flight of stone steps set into it. Bullying
the big stones uphill through the garden, like Sisyphus,
smashing irreplaceable plantings as I went and emitting
the requisite grunts and curses, I meditated upon how
much heavier these brutes had become since I dragged
them into the garden twenty years earlier.

Farther afield, we had an additional source of granite
boulders; we originally unearthed them when creating
the vegetable garden and then employed them to build a
raised strawberry planter along the driveway. Long since
abandoned, the planter had become a weedy eyesore. The
boulders, roughly the size of big watermelons, were pried
loose, heaved into a wheelbarrow, and transported about
two hundred feet to the site. (We have made it a first principle of our garden design to never have vehicle access
to locations where heavy materials need to be delivered.)
Getting round-shouldered boulders to sit securely on top
of one another to a height of more than five feet requires
immense finesse and an extensive vocabulary of profani-
ties and vulgarisms.

Marvelously, as the rock-wall level began to rise, I realized that I was constructing a far greater thing than we
had known. What was emerging slowly on the hilltop was
in fact a dolmen, from the old Cornish name, meaning lit-
erally "hole of stone." We'd visited several magnificent dol-
mens in Ireland, great mounds of stone with passage tombs
deep in their interior. Well, all right then, that was more

like it. This wasn't just some moronic pile of stones I was amassing, this was a construction whose roots stretched back to the megalithic stoneworks of prehistory.

The rubble to fill the core of the promontory I set to wheelbarrowing in from increasingly great distances. Belatedly, I had realized that it was in alarmingly short supply. Not long before, the whole place was rubble; now there was barely a decent bit of fill to be found on the property. I drove down to the ferry landing and, beneath the curious gaze of tourists, filled our van with five-gallon buckets of crushed oystershell and pebble. But for all my effort, the amount of fill was insignificant. There happened to be a large number of glass jars and bottles in our recycling box, and I was struck with the serendipitous realization that if I were to bury a layer of these at the bottom of the dolmen, covered with layers of cobbles, the nooks and crannies thus formed would make a perfect hibernaculum for overwintering garter snakes. A dolmen and a hibernaculum both—the genius of the thing was breathtaking. Renewed enthusiasm even justified having a dump truck load of fill brought in by our neighbor Dave. Paying top dollar for sand and gravel planes cruelly against the grain, but it did save endless hours of digging and hauling and subsequent lamentations over aching knees and ankles.

Finally completed, the new rock feature was a marvel, mirroring the stone walls and stairways below it while elevating us onto a pedestal of self-congratulation. For all its madness, the project reinforced a familiar lesson—that gardening is primarily a matter of doing, rather than of sitting and looking at what's been done, no matter from how grand a vantage point.

But the story doesn't end there. Stones have ways of their own, ancient inclinations and angles of repose unknown to human inquiry. In the course of maneuvering pieces out of the garden, I had come upon a particularly fine sandstone specimen about five feet long and irregularly shaped to about eighteen inches wide. Recognizing its suitability as a standing stone, we decided to install it as a focal point partway up the hill. I wrestled it to the path, where I hoped to somehow load it into the wheelbarrow. Unable to pick it up, I heaved the stone by this end and that, trying without success to bully it into the barrow. Nothing worked. The stone was as determined not to go into the barrow as I was determined that it should. It had become a *mano a litho* thing. I stood the stone on end, my arms around it as though embracing a frigid lover, and tried to waltz it headfirst into the barrow. Suddenly I was thrown violently backward onto the ground, the stone thumping down alongside me. Had it fallen on me, instead, there'd be less of me here to tell the tale. But the stone had merely been stubborn, not vindictive, and I realized that its ancient determination was vastly more powerful than my own. The stone had spoken. It had thrown me down to let me know that it wished to stand precisely where it was.

Not fool enough to contest the issue further, I raised the standing stone there, alongside our patio and pool, burying the heavier end in the ground and facing it toward a stone alcove. It stood impassively for a few days before we noticed the face. Once noticed, it was so unmistakable we wondered how we hadn't seen it instantly. The whole stone is a face—two deep-set eyes, high cheekbones, a Roman nose, a mouth opened as though for song or scream. It looks uncannily at times like Edvard Munch's *The Scream.* Depending upon the angle of sunlight, its expression of sadness or terror metamorphoses into something warmer, some form of ancient, stony wisdom and compassion.

Let me be clear: the face was not chiseled by human hands; nor is it an imaginative construct, the way we perceive images in passing clouds or the glowing embers of a fire. The face exists within the stone and the stone stands where it does, expressing the emotions it does for reasons of its own. Installing it had been a fairly simple task compared with the new arbor or the vantage point, yet this particular construction is in many ways the most complex, and certainly most mysterious, of any in the garden.

Gardening with the
Goddess of Fire

THE GARDENER ABROAD is a quizzical creature, mar-
veling at gorgeous gardens visited, anxious to identify almost-familiar plants, perhaps piqued with
envy over the nonchalance with which tender specimens
can be cultivated in foreign climes. For the Canadian
gardener—whose defining genius is, after all, outwitting
winter weather—a visit to the tropics can be especially
unsettling, as I confirmed during a midwinter camping
trip on the Big Island of Hawaii.

Sandy and I chose the Big Island because it has lots of
open space and a stunning spectrum of ecosystems. We
had a full month to ramble through paradise. Our enthusiasm sailed buoyantly above news reports, mere weeks
before our departure, showing the Big Island deluged by
torrential rain. Bridges and sections of road were swept

away, leaving campers stranded for days. Abandoning their swamped tents, they huddled miserably all night in campground washrooms. We were forewarned: camping—not to mention gardening—in Hawaii, though full of earthly delights, is not for the faint of heart.

We were barely off the plane, swathed in balmy air, before being swarmed by blooming bougainvillea. Bougainvillea everywhere—sheared as shrubs, tumbling down banks, climbing high into trees and in outrageous shades of crimson, bronzy orange, rose pink, pale yellow, pure white, and more. Orchids growing wild in ditches. Camellias at every corner. Poinsettias, six feet high, massed in full bloom along roadsides, a dazzling mockery of northerners' pre-Christmas secreting of scrawny potted plants in closets in order to force a few blooms. Whole yards of red hot pokers bloomed so unabashedly they'd constitute a bylaw infraction in many Canadian municipalities. Enormous agaves grew in succulent clusters, with flowering stalks like space-age spires. Grasses, too, from giants with flamboyant flowering stems catching sunlight in pink and red and bronze panicles down to miniature tufted grasses that would be divine in your scree back home. The foliage plants were so fulsome you could weep—brilliantly variegated understory shrubs, lacy tree ferns and giant-leafed bananas, palm trees and tremendous spreading banyan and monkeypod trees.

It all seemed too much. Too too. At one point Sandy and I found ourselves in a public garden, mesmerized by a huge, blooming bird of paradise bush while being ravished by the fragrance of nearby gardenia blossoms. Amid such extremities of plant life one's gardening parameters implode. The agonizing one does back home over acceptable color combinations is blown away in a poof! as one stands agog among preposterously vivid splashes of color. In this light, this environment, they work perfectly, like garish aloha shirts no one with a shred of decency would be caught dead wearing back home.

Nevertheless, there's a deep-rooted psychological need to make linkages with the familiar, and every peculiar plant we encountered we decided must be a distant relative of something we grow ourselves. That perennial with tall flowering stems was terribly reminiscent of our *Gaura lindheimeri,* and those mysterious broad-leafed shrubs surely were a type of rhododendron. Trying to identify hundreds of hitherto unknown species is a particular fixation of the gardener abroad. Quickly the choice becomes clear: either stay out of parks and gardens altogether, or acquire a reliable field guide and devote your holiday to looking up obscure plant names, rather than heading to the beaches for snorkeling, surfing, and boogie-boarding.

The glories of Hawaiian gardens are not matched in the campground department. Starting on the wrong foot by ignoring signs about camping without a permit, we spent the first night sleeping in our economy rental car at a remote park populated with several battalions of feral cats. In the middle of the night we were jolted awake by a cop shining a flashlight in our faces. Well, actually, no, we didn't have a permit; we'd tried to obtain one, dutiful

Canadians that we are, but it being Thanksgiving weekend, the county office that issues camping permits was closed. Somehow this was our fault. Chastened, next morning we sped back to the park office in Kailua. Naturally, the office was still closed.

Undeterred, we headed south down the Kona coast through a marvelous landscape of blooming hibiscus, bougainvillea, orchids, and poinsettias. Exotic scents enveloped us. Hillside coffee plantations stretched down to brilliant seascapes. At another county office we booked a few days' stay at a "quiet, remote" beach park in Ka'u district. Site of an abandoned wharf that had served the island's once-thriving sugar cane industry, this little park looked beautifully forlorn. A row of small shelters was occupied by native Hawaiians, most of whom remained huddled around a television all day watching decrepit American sitcoms. We pitched our tent in the windswept field. A park attendant came over to warn us against fraternizing with the natives, as though we were a pair of Edwardian twits meandering through head-hunting country. As twilight descended through the palm trees, carloads of Hawaiians came rumbling into the parking lot. A party began, featuring the consumption of astonishing volumes of beer and the loud playing of schmaltzy Hawaiian music on car stereos. The festivities ended abruptly at about 8 PM, when everyone lay down on the grass and fell asleep. Not exactly the hula-and-luau extravaganzas to be seen at luxury hotels, this event seemed somehow more authentically Hawaiian. We, too, drifted into contented slumber.

Awakening to the singing of tropical birds and a golden sunrise through palm trees, we spent the next several days snorkeling in nearby pools and exploring the region—the shoreline grasslands at Ka Lae, the black-sand beach at Punaluu, and, not to stray too far from horticulture, the arboretum at Manuka State Park.

Hilo, on the island's lush eastern side, is a waterfront town straight out of Joseph Conrad. There's a lovely thirty-acre waterfront park containing Lili'uokalani Gardens, one of the largest yedo-style Japanese gardens in the world and the largest formal Japanese garden found outside Japan. Laced with streams and carp ponds, the garden is dotted with pagodas and stone lanterns and has a pagoda bridge, a Japanese teahouse, and a wooden torii gate. Named after the great Hawaiian monarch Queen Lili'uokalani, the park acknowledges the huge contribution to island life made by successive generations of Japanese.

Nearby we found the renowned farmers' market, where we loaded up on fresh papayas, avocados, pineapples, and sweet, small bananas at giveaway prices. Several gardeners I spoke with noted how the trade winds sprinkling moisture every once in a while, generally at night, make watering largely unnecessary. No need to water, no fear of frost, rich volcanic soil: it's understandable if you begin to resent the arduousness of gardening at home.

As though to stoke the fires of resentment, we stopped in at Nani Mau Gardens, a large, Japanese-style show garden near Hilo, its name meaning "forever beautiful" in Hawaiian. And indeed all the elements of beauty were present: brightly colored tropical birds singing in the tree-tops, banks of spectacular flowers and foliage, and more exotic fragrances than a department-store fragrance shop. Palm trees grew throughout the garden. The anthurium grove featured masses of orange, white, pink, and red anthuriums, grown in the traditional manner in the shade of Hawaiian hapuu tree ferns. The ginger garden contained a diversity of ginger plants with fabulous shapes and colors and heady fragrances. Masses of show orchids were cleverly arranged around a series of small waterfalls. By the time we swooned into the hibiscus garden we were dangerously close to sensory overload. The Nani Mau fruit orchard had an impressive display of traditional Polynesian staples such as breadfruit, noni fruit, and kuki nuts, along with litchis, mulberries, oranges, soursops, and star fruit. On a little knoll swathed in golden bamboo stood a lovely Japanese bell tower built from twenty thousand boards without the use of a single screw or nail. Struck with a suspended pole, the huge bell reverberated with a resonance that seemed to call us all to daily meditation.

But where was everybody? The parking lot entertained a regular stream of cars and tour buses, but there was seldom anyone to be seen in the garden itself—except when the tram swooshed by. Yes, "Forever Beautiful" had a twenty-minute, narrated tram tour, "an enlightening and educational experience" as well as "a great way for young and old alike to explore this tropical paradise." And that's precisely what young and old alike were doing. Passengers disembarking from a tour bus piled onto the tram and were whizzed around the gardens with stops at strategic spots for "must have" photo opportunities. Having glossed over the garden's possibilities, the visitors trundled into the gift shop to view the "exclusive" gifts and souvenirs, then proceeded to the Island Buffet lunch at the garden restaurant and perhaps a bit of pampering at the Nani Mau Salon and Spa. Ah, garden touring—there's no life like it!

Skipping the souvenir shop and the beauty salon, we headed south to the fabled Red Road in Puna district. We pitched camp at a state park located in a murky ironwood grove along a rocky shoreline. The campground was deserted. Not surprisingly, because the roads were rutted almost to impassability, the overflowing garbage cans were ripe with the stench of tropical decay, and the pit toilets were, let's say, less than fastidiously maintained. An air of desolation hung about the place. Mongooses slinking like furtive gangsters near the jungle's edge disappeared into its gloom when we drew too close. Introduced to Hawaii in a misguided attempt to control rats in the sugar cane fields, these predators have been decimating indigenous bird populations ever since. Our guidebook noted that this park is not popular at night, because ghosts of old Hawaiians are believed to wander there.

Undeterred by squalor or specters, and feeling ever so superior to the tour-bus and four-star-hotel crowd, we spent the happy hour on the cliff-tops, gazing across a Pacific uncluttered from there to Antarctica. Reclining on camp chairs, tremendous surf surging beneath us, the sun descending through a haze of pink while a brilliant moon rose, we sipped chilled wine and nibbled hors d'oeuvres.

It rapidly grew dark. I flicked on the flashlight, only to see that we were being swarmed by enormous cockroaches. Hundreds upon hundreds of the supersized brown beasts were crawling at our feet. Waves of biophobia washing over us, we grabbed our gear and stumbled up the hill to our campsite. But the roaches were massed there, too. The campground, it soon became apparent, was one vast breeding ground for cockroaches. They got into our food, they got into the car, they got into the tent. Sandy awoke to long antennae flickering softly on her face. Too fast to be caught by hand and cast out, this interloper met its end from a crunching right hook.

Bidding a premature farewell to fabled Red Road, we headed north up the spectacular Hamakua coast, past beautiful coves and across dramatic ravines. We ended up at a state recreation area, a charming spot on the northeastern slopes of massive Mauna Kea, with tropical forest, expansive lawns, and a marvelous hibiscus collection. Now we were back on the right horticultural path. Again, the park was deserted except for ourselves. Each of the three campsites had a covered shelter with concrete floor—handy during the frequent rains here on the windward side—and we pitched our tent in one.

Next morning, as stiff as your proverbial board, I ventured into the washroom and stripped down for a bracing cold-water shower. But yech! The floor and walls of the shower stall were crawling with thousands of small, white maggots. Balled masses of them seethed in every corner, wriggling a hideous hula to disease and death. The jovial park attendant doused the showers with enough chlorine to kill a sperm whale, but next morning the maggots were back, and subsequent showers involved body contortions worthy of a Kundalini yoga master.

Undaunted, we set about exploring the Hamakua coast—picturesque waterfalls, charming small towns, two excellent botanical gardens—and the nearby dramatic ranching country around Waimea. No matter where on the globe you're wandering, it's a treat to come upon a place into which some mad-keen gardener has poured heart and soul (and as often as not the family's life savings as well). The Hawaii Tropical Botanical Garden is one of those places. A few miles up the coast from Hilo lies a little sheltered valley named Onomea (meaning "the best place"). Inspired by its secluded beauty, two vacationing Americans, Dan and Pauline Lutkenhouse, in 1977 bought a twenty-acre waterfront parcel with only the vaguest notion of what they might do with it. Dan owned a trucking business in San Francisco, and neither of them had any horticultural training. Never mind: the notion of creating a tropical botanical garden took hold, and, as every true-blue gardener knows, once a notion has taken hold, there's no escaping it. Like moths to the flame, they sold their business and moved to Hawaii to get down to serious gardening.

The little valley was in those days overgrown with invasive trees, vines, shrubs, and weeds. Dan spent the next eight years, seven days a week, clearing the jungle by hand, so as not to disturb the native plants. He and a couple of helpers eradicated the invasives, laid out pathways, cleared streamways and waterfalls, hand dug ponds and a small lake, and brought in plants from endangered tropical jungles around the world. Now, with more than two thousand species represented, the garden functions as "a plant sanctuary, a living seed bank, and a study center for trees and plants of the tropical world."

Here we saw tiger and butterfly orchids, heliconias, and more than eighty varieties of bromeliads, mostly from the jungles of South America. There's Amazon lily and Indonesian ginger, Madagascar travelers trees, purple lotus, giant monkeypod trees, African tulip trees with vivid orange blossoms, stilt root palms, the lemon bay rum tree from Trinidad. Groves of giant tree ferns, sword ferns, and ancient cycads recreate prehistoric forests. The garden's collection of Hawaiian endemic plants—many of them threatened—includes the rare palm *Pritchardia schattauerii*, Molokai's loulu palm, and the thorny floss silk tree. "We're preserving the valley so that mankind can enjoy it forever," Dan Lutkenhouse said, his passion amplified to Wagnerian intensity. "I believe that we should all try to leave the world a better place than we found it."

The next good place we found was Hawaii Volcanoes National Park, encompassing 520 square miles, descending from gigantic Mauna Loa's summit at 13,677 feet to the remote south coast. The park's rugged beauty and steaming volcanoes provide a timely reminder that the Big Island is home to Pele, goddess of fire, who resides in one of the active volcanoes that periodically send lava flows pouring downhill, destroying everything in their path. Such was the sad fate of the Kalapana Gardens and Royal Gardens subdivisions here, obliterated by lava flows in 1990 and now buried under some thirty feet of solid rock. Talk about gardening under adverse conditions.

After an entrancing drive down a road winding through golden grasses and young trees, we pitched our tent in an alcove of small shrubs in a primitive campground well off the beaten track. The landscape was ropy lava, called pahoehoe, polished bronze by wind and rain and colonized by desert plants, particularly native grasses. From this sanctuary we ventured forth to tramp the park's great hiking trails, through tropical rain forests, deserts, grasslands, and surreal moonscapes of lava flows and steam vents.

We spent our final week on the Kona coast at a beach park several miles down a tortuous hillside road. The crescent beach in a lovely, cliff-rimmed setting was hopping with kids cavorting in the surf, bikini queens striding the strand, and spinner dolphins flashing silver in the bay. Perfection. Sleeping peacefully in our tent on the beach, we were again startled awake by a flashlight. Yes, we had a permit. Yes, Kennedy. Yes. Good night. Good night. I drifted back to sleep pondering the folly of human systems, and then *wham!* was jolted awake again, this time by the crashing sound of an onrushing tsunami. Only it wasn't a tsunami, just the surf; because the shorelines along these volcanic islands drop sharply, waves can break with tremendous impact. I lay awake for hours, remembering the story we'd been told of a group of people who camped on a coastal plain near here. A sudden earthquake dislodged huge lava boulders on the cliffs behind them, sending the boulders bounding downhill. Terrified, the campers fled toward the shore for escape, only to have the shoreline drop away. A tsunami, triggered by the earthquake, dragged them out to sea, then cast them back up on shore. Miraculously, only two campers died.

Earthquakes, tsunamis, volcanic lava flows—who in their right mind would garden in such an unstable place? Still, gardeners are gardeners, and you'll find them planting in even the newest earth on Earth. On one of our last days we visited a forlorn-looking subdivision laid out over top of a recent lava flow. Crumpled black lava stretched in all directions, as though we were standing inside a gigantic barbecue. Amid this desolation, gardeners were busy piling lava blocks into rock walls, terracing and laying down pathways, and planting trees and shrubs right in the volcanic clinkers: gambling, one supposes, that Pele will turn her fiery attentions elsewhere for the foreseeable future. The American writer Eleanor Perenyi noted that "to garden is to let optimism get the better of judgment," and there are few examples more extreme than these brave souls who would garden with the goddess of fire.

The Ten Commandments

B Y WAY OF a cautionary meditation on the gardening life, it may be instructive to cast our minds back to the Old Testament, to the Book of Deuteronomy and muddled old Moses stumbling around in the mountains and receiving from on high the Ten Commandments. Scrupulously avoiding any sacrilegious inclinations, we may then review the Ten Commandments of Gardening, examining our hearts to determine which of them we're obeying and which not, mindful that only through adherence to these precepts can we hope to retain the true purity of horticultural passion.

At a glance, the first commandment might not seem to hold any relevance for gardening: "I am the Lord thy God, which brought thee out of the land of Egypt, from the house of bondage. Thou shalt have none other gods before me." Examining the matter more closely, however, we realize it's undoubtedly correct that by taking up gardening one escapes the house of bondage—letting dirty dishes pile up in the sink and dust-balls grow to the size of tumbleweeds—to get on with more pressing matters in the yard. But, as every calloused-palmed gardener knows, we haven't escaped bondage as a lifestyle so much as exchanged the indoor house of bondage for the outdoor garden of bondage. And it could be argued that being a slave to the garden is the more arduous of the two, that gardening at its most extreme is cruel and unusual punishment that would enrage Amnesty International if it ever got wind of it.

As for having no other gods, I take this as instruction for gardeners to abandon reckless daydreams about taking up a hobby or going off on an extended trip somewhere. Make no mistake about it: gardeners who take up bowling or decide to kayak the canals of Europe will come to a bad end. We have neither the time nor the aptitude for distractions and merriment, save perhaps the occasional watching of a Home & Garden Television show. Special dispensations are available if an overseas jaunt can be shown to be a bona fide plant-collecting expedition, but in general, when it comes to having fun, gardeners are better advised to stick with turning the compost heaps.

The first commandment goes on about "Thou shalt not make thee any graven image, or any likeness of any thing that is in heaven above, or that is in the earth beneath, or that is in the waters beneath the earth." It's hard to imagine that even the most craven collector of kitsch could interpret this commandment as anything other than an admonition concerning the folly of the graven images some of us insist on dragging into our gardens—gnomes and fairies on toadstools, mermaids and fake turtles in the pool, concrete fawns with enormous limpid eyes, Silly Frogs made out of "high quality plastic," inflatable great horned owls, and, perhaps most regrettable of all, Dung Bunny Poo Pets. These cannot be explained away as artistic touches; they are an abomination that even horticultural agnostics must learn to eschew.

Certain gardeners are masters of situational ethics in this matter. You must keep that ceramic hedgehog, because it was given to you by the grandkids at Christmas and they'd be terribly hurt if it went missing. And you couldn't possibly throw out that corpulent stone toad that your mother used to love so much. We tuck these tacky attachments under the hosta leaves, attempt to camouflage them amid the ligularias, lest our high-blown horticultural companions spot them and we're publicly exposed. No other gods, my friends, and, please, for decency's sake, no graven images.

The second commandment suffers from none of the equivocation of the first: "Thou shalt not take the name of the Lord thy God in vain." This is something I've wanted to address within the gardening community for quite some time now. I refer to the astonishing amount of cursing and swearing that erupts in even the most genteel of gardens. Notwithstanding that allowances must be made in the matter of malignant garden sprayers, do you think it's necessary, for example, when you yank out one of your prized seedlings, absent-mindedly mistaking it for a weed, to greet the occasion with a streak of expletives that even the most depraved blasphemer would delete? Is it too much to ask that you do your pruning of climbing and rambling roses without multiple shrieks of "For fuck's sakes!" and "Let go of me, you filthy bastard!" ringing out across the garden every five minutes? Calling down curses upon your secateurs, misplaced somewhere in the shrubbery, isn't going to help you locate them. Has it not occurred to you that the reason the lawnmower won't start after several dozen vigorous yanks on the cord is that you have failed to maintain and service it correctly, or that the gas tank is empty, rather than that the machine itself is, as is shouted between repeated vicious kicks, a stupid, goddamn worthless piece of shite?

The third commandment is: "Six days thou shalt labor, and do all thy work: But the seventh day is the sabbath... in it thou shalt not do any work." This commandment, perhaps more than any other, conclusively demonstrates that Jehovah of the Old Testament, notwithstanding all the backstory about the Garden of Eden, was no gardener. Refraining from working on Sundays is a commandment not even the most pious of gardeners can be expected to obey. Nevertheless, it can be a useful psychological stratagem in the relentless give-and-take of certain gardening households. It can, for example, be cited chapter and verse as a compelling reason *not* to get outdoors and lend a hand with cleaning the pool or dividing the perennials on the weekend.

You'll also find some Sunday gardeners attempting to justify themselves by claiming that transplanting gargantuan root-balls isn't work at all, because it's so much fun, and anyway, they're not getting paid for it. "This is my form of relaxation!" they'll grunt as they're staggering uphill with a barrowload of boulders that would stymie a bulldozer. Let's be honest: the average gardener would as soon be condemned to the eternal flames of hell as give up Sunday gardening.

Which gets us to the fourth commandment: "Honor thy father and thy mother." This would be a lot easier to do if only thy father and thy mother didn't talk so much about their own gardening accomplishments, implying that you'll never do as well yourself, no matter how hard you try. Or, worse, insist on lauding your sister's garden to the skies while never saying a kind word about yours. "Yes, your sister has that, too," Mother says as she points out one of your finest specimens, with that telltale trace of disapproval in her tone, "but I find it's so much more effective how she's used it in mass plantings. This solitary specimen you've got," and here she grimaces painfully, "looks rather lonely and forlorn, don't you agree?" No, you don't agree in the least—your sister's garden is a hopeless muddle, not even

in the same league as your chef d'oeuvre—but you bite
your tongue and say nothing. For your birthday, dear old
Mom and Pop give you a copy of *Gardening for Dummies.*
"Just a joke, dear," they laugh, "but there are some useful
tips in there, too!"

Needless to say, this particular commandment takes
on greater resonance over time. Once your own kids have
grown up and planted gardens of their own, you're thinking it wouldn't kill them to do a bit more honoring of your
hard-won horticultural expertise. You find yourself passing
on advice, but never in the irritating way your own parents
did. No, you try show interest in xeriscaping and nature-
scaping and all these other ridiculous fads your kids are
involved in. But where's the gratitude, I ask you? Where's
the honoring of thy father and thy mother?

Perhaps most problematic of all is the fifth commandment: "Thou shalt not kill." You know as well as I do that
if gardeners ever took this commandment to heart, plant
sales would plummet, the garden supply business would
grind to a halt, and nurseries would declare bankruptcy as
frequently as airlines. Fortunately, no such crisis is immi-
nent, because if there's one thing gardeners are good at,
it's the sustained and systematic killing of plants. "Oh, I
don't know what happened!" they exclaim over some poor,
wizened runt of a plant now gasping its last. "It looked
fine when I bought it. I did everything right, but then
the leaves all turned brown and fell off. Do you think I've
killed it?" Of course you've killed it, you ninny; you've been
killing plants all your life. But the remarkable thing is, no

matter how many innocent victims a gardener has managed to butcher over the years, each new death still comes as a great surprise.

This habitual killing of plants by gardeners remains a secret that is never mentioned in polite society. Instead, gardeners collude to blame every conceivable factor for a plant's death except their own negligence. Unscrupulous plant breeders and nurserymen. Toxic fertilizers. Global warming. The lunar cycle. The positioning of the stars. Almost anything imaginable could have caused this pitiful plant's demise. Anything except you. Anything except the naked truth that you bought it from a hothouse, brought it home, and planted it out on the coldest day of the year without a moment's hardening off. Or you left it sitting for hours in a locked car in full sunshine on the hottest day of the year.

And here we must consider the wonderful gardening advice-givers on radio, who so graciously ignore the fact that most of the people calling in are horticultural homicidal maniacs. These listeners drown plants with compulsive watering. They dig plants up and then leave them lying on the driveway while they go in for lunch and have a nap. They prune plants back to woody little stumps, then think it's most peculiar that no new buds are appearing. They bury plants up to their necks in sand, then pour sackfuls of 20-20-20 on them." Oh, I'm afraid I may have lost it," they'll say about some mangled victim of their ministrations.

You'd expect that the gardening experts, forced to listen repeatedly to this litany of vegecide, would deal firmly with the culprits. But nothing of the sort. "No, you've done everything just right," they'll purr, in their perfect radio voices. "Maybe give it a bit of a copper spray and a top-dressing of well-rotted manure, and it'll green up nicely for you in no time." Surely this is extending the permissive society to impermissible limits. Has our faith in the gurus been misplaced? Is it possible that our experts, eminent and admired as they may be, respond with indulgence because they know better than most that if we didn't have this cadre of dedicated plant killers hard at it day and night—and, yes, I confess I'm one of them; I recently tortured and killed a *Pieris japonica* with a criminal negligence that should get me twenty-five years to life, if there were any justice in this world, which there is not—if we didn't have this bottomless pit into which plants are ceaselessly tossed by homicidal gardeners, the horticultural industry would stagnate? There'd be no growth, no expansion, no progress. And then where would we be, eh?

The sixth commandment, as I'm certain no gardener needs to be reminded, is: "Neither shalt thou commit adultery." And while we may all suppose that a bit of adultery every now and then would be fun enough in its own way, really, I ask you: Who's got the time? Plus, you'd have to change out of your gardening gear into sexy clothes. Is your hair right, or are there still twigs and leaves caught in it? Certainly you'd have to pick up on the personal hygiene end of things; *please!* get the soil out from under those fingernails. And after all that, there you'd be, thrashing away in sweaty sheets in a dreary motel room somewhere, the whole time worrying over whether your meconopsis are drying out. Where you should by rights be having enormous fun, experimenting with positions you've never even heard of and pinching naughty buttocks, you're just going through the motions, desperately aware that the fuchsias need to be pinched back. Most adulterous gardeners are doomed to coitus interruptus and a quick dash back to the languishing dahlias. All things considered, gardening and adultery are not a satisfactory match.

But the same certainly can't be said about the seventh commandment: "Neither shalt thou steal." Some gardeners are almost as accomplished at stealing as they are at killing. You watch them strolling the grounds of a public garden or, in the most brazen cases, even private gardens. Observe the peculiar twitching movements of the hand. The subtle fondling of seed heads or fresh shoots. The casual checking to see if anyone's watching. The furtive movement to the pocket or the purse as seeds or softwood slips are surreptitiously secreted away. They're smiling and bantering jovially with their companions, pointing out a lovely arrangement over there, a clever combination over here, while the furtive hand goes about its nefarious work with the calculating agility of a seasoned shoplifter. Of course these light-fingered gardeners would never think of themselves as common thieves; their purposes are so much more noble and refined, aligned as they are with the higher attainments of horticulture, but it's petty theft nevertheless.

Then there are the demolition site experts, who specialize in "rescuing" plants from yards whose buildings are scheduled to be knocked down. Long before the wrecking ball and the bulldozers show up, these types have their eye on certain choice specimens. The legitimate occupants of the doomed house are scarcely out the door—sometimes they're not even out the door—before enlightened plant rescuers descend on the place and set to tearing the yard apart like agitated idiots on some "reality gardening" TV show. Notwithstanding the gold-rush haste of these sorties, their motivations too have a cast of nobility about them—the preserving for posterity of venerable old specimens. This being the case, it's difficult to determine why the rescue missions are so frequently carried out under cover of darkness.

You'll see other purloining plantspersons at the bulb bins in the nursery. Over in the connoisseur narcissi section there'll be Lemon Beauty at five bulbs for $8.50. The thieving gardener will put twelve bulbs in her bag, then mark it as ten, certain that the harried clerk at the cash register isn't going to take them out and count them. If a suspicious clerk should in fact catch him out, the thief will coolly feign indifference. "Oh, nine, ten, eleven— really, what difference does it make? We're talking mere pennies here." Mere pennies indeed. Even more shockingly, some grasping gardeners will fill a bag with connoisseur narcissi, then mark the bulbs as King Alfreds, which cost a quarter as much. Those who've really sunk into the pit of depravity will fill a bag with amaryllis bulbs, worth thirteen bucks apiece, and try to pass them off as unusually large King Alfreds.

Perhaps it's the prevalence of such persons within the gardening community that accounts for the fact that the last three commandments all address problems associated with the neighbors. Which makes us wonder whether Jehovah—notwithstanding the nonsense about working on Sundays—might have been a gardener after all. As every gardener knows, a good neighbor is a treasure beyond reckoning. To have next door a compatible spirit, a person of conscientious temperament and elevated perception, is at least as precious as any prized perennial. Conversely, an inconsiderate neighbor can leech the joy out of even a well-loved garden. Habitually barking dogs, screaming televisions, roaring automobiles, and fractious arguments over property lines, fence heights, hedge maintenance, or overhanging trees can turn what should be a haven into hell.

The eighth commandment is: "Neither shalt thou bear false witness against thy neighbor." This would be an easier commandment to observe if your neighbors were even half as considerate as you yourself are. And most particularly, if they had the sense to recognize that your garden is by far the finest one in the neighborhood, one they would do well to study in order to improve their own modest efforts.

Unfortunately, most people lack the perspective to accomplish this. They're too preoccupied, I suppose, with breaking all of the commandments of gardening. Just looking at their hyacinth shows each spring tells you exactly who's been pilfering bulbs at the neighborhood nursery. They don't have the decency to tuck their plastic frogs and gnomes under the hostas and ligularias; some of them don't even have hostas and ligularias. I mean, a dash of false witness isn't going to do these Philistines any harm. And talk about taking the name of the Lord in vain. Really, the language being flung about some of these yards would scandalize a longshoreman. Watching the peculiar comings and goings at very unusual hours, I wouldn't be surprised, either, to learn that the neighborhood is a seething hotbed of adultery. Who knows, maybe it's by way of cover-up that they have to march out and mow their lawns on Sunday morning, while you're trying to keep holy the Lord's day with a bit of meditative weeding. They shout merrily back and forth over the roar of their mowers. Then they're out with the weed eaters and the leaf blowers, and flinging Weed & Feed on their lawns every five minutes, sprinklers splashing away on the sidewalks, while you're bringing your water-wise xeriscaping to a pitch of perfection. The color combinations some of them come up with don't bear mentioning, and if I see one more bed of marigolds and petunias I swear I'll retch. These crackpots are forever having people over to see their gardens, such as they are, barbecuing steaks and drinking wine and generally carrying on as though the whole thing were one big joke. Some of them have the audacity to engage you in gardening conversations, as though their quaint little places had anything in common with your masterpiece. Every so often, one of them will dare to offer you gardening advice—did you ever hear the likes of it! Oh no, I think it's perfectly legitimate to bear all the false witness you can against these nutcases.

The ninth commandment is: "Neither shalt thou desire thy neighbor's wife." Since we've already dealt with the issue of adultery, and since for years you've observed thy neighbor's wife put her cat out every morning so that it can come over and defecate in your vegetable beds, she wearing the same old slippers and pilled housecoat and with curlers in her hair, we have to assume that the desiring in question here pertains to matters other than lust. And there is something to this, because, no matter what else you might think about them, you have to admit that some of these neighbors' wives are pretty damned handy in the garden. You see them out there planting and pruning and tidying up for hours on end, in all types of weather. It's like having Rosie the Riveter next door, the way they're forever building new sheds and laying down patio pavers and espaliering fruit trees. Watching them go at it, I'm convinced some of these neighbor's wives are hard-wired for weeding. Meanwhile, their husbands are lolling in chaise lounges reading the sports pages and having the wife fetch them another cold beer in between her chores.

You compare those guys' lives of leisure with your own situation, dutifully trudging along in the garden, following the instructions growled at you by your own dear companion, and you do perhaps begin to desire thy neighbor's wife just a little. What a wonderful thing to have a wife who

tends the plants perfectly, cultivates gorgeous fruits, vegetables, and herbs, then whisks them indoors and whips up
gourmet organic meals that she serves you at a splendidly
decorated table. In short, a Martha Stewart sort of wife
(minus the insider trading, of course). A Lynda Reeves
kind of wife, a Debbie Travis style of wife. Ah! The dutiful husband drifts off in a dream of being coddled by such
a domestic diva. But suddenly he's jolted to attention by
marital reality. "Yes, dear? What's that? No, no, darling, no,
I wasn't daydreaming. Yes, I know we've got a ton of things
to get done. Yes, I'll get right on that job, just as soon as
I've finished picking up the cat excrement. Yes, love you
too, darling..."

The tenth, and mercifully last, commandment is: "Neither shalt thou covet thy neighbor's house...or any thing
that is thy neighbor's." And of course you wouldn't, if they
didn't make such a brazen show of their stuff. Every time
you get the stepladder out and climb up to peek through
the gap in the hedge, there's something new on display,
something trendy, something too terribly cutting-edge.
At your place, you're content to sit on the patio on folding
lawn chairs from the hardware store; but not the neighbors. Oh, no. They loll about on a pair of reproduction
Edwardian steamer chairs and a Monet-inspired bench
made of plantation teak. Your patio plants look lovely in
black plastic pots, but the neighbors have to have an osten-
tatious display of handmade terra cotta urns from Andalu-
cia. They can't resist mentioning their terra cotta Vicenza
urn, derived from the bronze mortars and pestles made

in Italy during the Renaissance, don't you know. While you're trying to get on with pruning the confounded wisteria for the tenth time this summer, they'll be leaning on the fence trying to chat you up about their reproduction Victorian terra cotta edging tile and their reproduction Victorian lead and glass cloches. And the outfits they're wearing! Traditional garden galoshes, socks in brown wool, immaculate brown cord trousers and linen shirt, goatskin work gloves. Can you imagine? They're invariably carrying a woven willow trug, in which they keep a designer weeding fork and a carbon steel rockery trowel with ash handle and a French watering can of hot-dipped galvanized steel, which you have to admit looks a bit fancier than your green plastic watering can from your local big-box department store. For the hundredth time, they draw your attention to their sundial in slate with hand-carved Celtic designs and their armillary and pedestal made of hand-ground and hand-polished steel.

You respond politely but unenthusiastically. Finally they get the message and go back to mowing their weedless lawn with their state-of-the-art, environmentally correct, high-tech, silent push mower. You glance for a moment at your own garden's *pièce de résistance*—a pair of resin-bonded cast-stone piglets that cost you an arm and a leg down at the home-reno store—and suddenly, plangently, something gives way deep within your spirit. Pathetically, you succumb to silent weeping as a tidal wave of coveting your neighbor's goods washes over you. You want their damned terra cotta Vicenza urns, their poncy reproduction Victorian lead and glass cloches, more than life itself. You are consumed with horrendous envy.

And this is what it comes to in the end for gardeners like you and me. Let's confess it openly: We've broken every commandment in the book. We've stolen shamelessly. Killed mercilessly. Coveted greedily. Maybe even dabbled in adultery. We are the horticultural equivalent of the Whores and the Beast of Babylon. Oh, woe!

But you know what? We'll get over it. We'll pick ourselves up, dust ourselves off, and get back into the fray with spirits bowed but unbroken. Because we know, you and I, in our heart of hearts, that there's another commandment, a higher commandment, and this one we obey without question. Yes, my friends, the eleventh commandment of gardening: Thou shalt not stop.

Darwin Was No Gardener

EOPLE IN THE know are forever telling us about the "evolution of gardens" and inviting us to take an imaginative stroll down the historical garden path, along which we might explore the styles and splendors of gardens through the ages. There's an exhilarating undercurrent in this concept, the notion that, from its beginnings in primal ooze, the garden gradually ascends in a dramatic progression, developing ever more complex and elaborate forms. Thus our green-thumbed ancestors begin in the misty innocence of the Garden of Eden and evolve over time through the Persian paradise garden, the nature mysticism of the Sino-Japanese garden, the medieval monastic herbarium, then ever onward through the rational Age of Enlightenment garden, the romantic landscapes of Capability Brown, the sexually ambivalent

Victorian fern grotto, the rhythmic landscapes of the New Wave school and all the rest: the thrilling implication being that these gardening styles eventually culminate in that pinnacle of design excellence now to be found manifest in my backyard and yours.

Breathtaking in its sweep, inspirational in its tone, this theory of garden evolution provides just the right motivational pop to get us outdoors in order to continue the Great Work. After a few seasons in the brutal proving grounds, however, the theory crumples completely. Almost any real-dirt gardener will recognize it as a concoction of whimsy and wishful thinking.

Talk of evolutionary theory immediately conjures the name Charles Darwin, long since canonized as the patron saint of evolutionism. The thesis I should like to advance is that Darwin—genius though he may have been—was, in fact, no gardener. His theory fits in a garden about as handsomely as an old toilet bowl raised on a plinth and planted with pelargoniums. Darwin is most celebrated for his book *On the Origin of Species by Means of Natural Selection,* which appeared in 1859. By "natural selection" he meant the fierce competition among organisms for space, food, and shelter. It is, he wrote, this jostling for the upper hand that enables some plants and animals to adapt and survive while others disappear. In a copse of young trees, for example, those that grow most rapidly survive. Slower growers, deprived of sunlight by their aggressive neighbors, become stunted, and die.

All well and good, no doubt, on the Galapagos Islands.

But not necessarily in a garden. For starters, the theory paints a bullish picture of organisms reproducing at an astonishing rate. This belies the fact that many gardeners spend a significant portion of each spring staring forlornly at germination trays in which nothing is producing at all. The few spindly seedlings that do eventually emerge hang on for a couple of days, then suffer a severe attack of damping-off, topple over, and expire. We're not talking here about survival of the fittest—we're talking about survival of anything.

As for the supposed fierce competition, in which less-well-adapted organisms falter and die, the theory fails entirely to account for the fact that the plant most likely to perish prematurely is the one you've paid the most money for. Or the one you've made the centerpiece of your garden. This is particularly true of trees. There's no conceit more doomed to hubris than that of designing a garden around a tree. The principal characteristic of these prima donna trees is, as we know, irrespective of species selected, once the whole garden is completed and all the underplantings are flourishing, the propensity to die. And not to die quickly, so as to get it over with and be replaced by a worthy successor. Rather to die in a slow, protracted, and painful way, often over several seasons, suspending the gardener in an agonizing state of uncertainty as to whether the tree is really dying or simply suffering from a malady whose cure will be revealed if only one maintains faith and patience. And so the tree lingers, gradually declining, casting its spectral pall over the garden.

But we gardeners are nothing if not loyal. Loyalty impels us to cherish a plant in good times and in bad. Not for us the whisking away of a problematic specimen merely because it's ailing a bit. Even less so on the flimsy pretext that it has fallen out of fashion, that superior forms are available, or any of the cant that slips so lubriciously from the lips of compulsive consumers. No, the loyal plantsperson acknowledges the sacredness of living things. He or she recognizes that, in taking on a plant—most especially trees, shrubs, and other long-lived sorts—one has entered into a relationship not to be casually discarded.

This was for many years precisely the attitude Sandy and I maintained toward a certain little eastern redbud, *Cercis canadensis,* that came to us as a foundling from the "clearance" corner of some long-forgotten nursery. The poor thing had plainly suffered neglect, and quite possibly abuse, early in life. Darwin might have condemned it to the trash can of adaptation, but not we. Promising it better days ahead, we planted it beside our new deck with an eye to someday lazing in its dappled shade.

The early years were not easy. The little tree was disinclined to grow, and what marginal growth it did attempt was invariably in a contrary direction. We came to recognize that it was afflicted with a fear of heights, a considerable disadvantage in a tree. Every spring I pruned it diligently, urging it toward the thirty-foot stature nature had ordained for it. Perversely, the puny trunk would zig to the left and get pruned, then zag to the right and get pruned again, resulting in a herringbone ascent that only a pathologically loyal arborist could love.

As the tree entered adolescence, we began to fret about its companions. Our planting scheme was founded on the venerable, if outdated, *Wyman's Gardening Encyclopedia*, which told us, "The Redbud is frequently used in combination with the Flowering Dogwood, for one augments the other, and they grow together over the same range from Florida to New England." Perfect. We'd plopped in a couple of pink-flowering dogwoods nearby. By the time it had grown to about ten feet, the redbud began to bloom, with tiny, magenta, pealike flowers clustered along its trunk and limbs. Alongside white-flowering dogwoods, the bloom would have had considerable charm. Instead, we had created a color clash that might rival a Jennifer Lopez gown on Oscar night. Still, we stayed the course. After the flowers had mercifully faded, we rejoiced in the "flicker light" produced by sunlight dappling through the tree's crown of heart-shaped leaves. In autumn the redbud's foliage turned a pleasing yellow. We were reaping our just rewards for having stood by the little *Cercis*.

As spring approached, however, we could no longer postpone replacing the rotting deck upon which the redbud had cast its welcome shade. Reflecting on the limited life span of wooden decks in our fungi- and bacteria-rich west coast climate, we opted for a patio, including a roofed area, an enlarged pond, and a number of other refinements. Our splendid redbud would sit smack in the middle. It never entered our minds to move the tree. No, we instead did everything possible to accommodate it. Our arboreal loyalty knew no limits.

One fateful evening, though, as we surveyed the job site, it came to us with the force of divine revelation: that redbud had to go. It no more belonged in the middle of a patio than it would have in the middle of the kitchen. I awoke the next morning at dawn and revisited the decision. There was no turning back. Bristling with spade and grub hoe, I excavated an enormous root-ball and levered the resistant tree out of the ground. I talked to it incessantly, muttering reassurances that all would be well. But as we wrestled, the redbud and I, like Jacob and the angel, I could hear the tree weeping.

The tree had truth on its side, as trees usually do, for *Wyman's* warns: "These are difficult to transplant, and the smaller they are when moved, the more likely they are to survive." We dragged the patient to a new location, and I planted it with guilt-laced love, pouring onto its roots a small fortune in root booster. Returning to the house, I was reminded that it was Good Friday morning and that one of the redbuds is called the Judas tree, from the legend that it was upon this tree that Judas Iscariot hanged himself after betraying Jesus of Nazareth in the Garden of Gethsemane. Following a further year of agony, our poor redbud was as dead as Judas himself.

Perhaps it is an abhorrence of such betrayal that drives so many gardeners into an excessive solicitude. How else to explain, for example, the compulsion some of us have for raising difficult monocarps? A monocarp is not a singular fish, but rather a plant that flowers only once, then dies. Behavior perfectly acceptable in annuals and biennials, but does the gardener need the burden of keeping a problematic plant alive, year after year, for an eventual blooming that will in all likelihood occur while she's away from home for the week?

The answer, of course, is yes.

We've had several such sluggards at our place. Hardy, drought-tolerant, native, and easily naturalized species are our stock in trade, except for the occasional oddity that comes to us as a gift from some generous gardener with an inflated sense of our expertise. One such gift was the tremendous lily *Cardiocrinum giganteum,* which is not a true lily at all, but closely related. A native of the Himalayas, it's frost-hardy, generally listed as zone 6, requiring shade or semi-shade and deep, humus-rich soil that is moist but well drained. "None too easy to grow," one of our manuals warned. Undaunted, I planted our young specimen in the shade cast by the summerhouse—one of the few spots in our garden that comes even remotely close to that mythical "moist yet well-drained" condition so favored by garden advice-givers.

For its first few years the plant resembled a hosta, bearing a basal rosette of large, glossy leaves. Like hostas, we soon discovered, *Cardiocrinum giganteum* is a favorite food of slugs, which gather in moist, shady places as reliably as Seattle-ites do at their favorite coffee shop. Thus ensued many tedious hours of picking slugs off the tattered leaves and questioning whether the effort was worthwhile. Then one July—lo and behold!—an enormous stalk emerged, soaring well over six feet high and bearing about twenty large, white flowers that looked like trumpet lilies and cast a sublime scent. Come evening, we'd lie down to sleep in the summerhouse, spirits soothed as we drifted away to dreamland on that divine fragrance. All too soon, heart-breakingly, the flowers faded and fell, to be followed by dramatic seed heads. In autumn, with the main bulb dead, we separated the small offsets and replanted them. Slugs permitting, they would have bloomed in another four years. But the slugs did not permit. They persisted, while the *Cardiocrinum* did not.

Another monocarp, *Echium pininana,* has a shorter but more demanding life cycle. A member of the borage family, native to the Canary Islands, it thrives in dry, poor soil, loves full sun, is supposedly excellent in seacoast gardens and self-seeds freely under ideal conditions. It is also half-hardy, that treacherous term that seduces you into growing things common sense—not to mention Darwin—warns you ought not, certainly not in our little frost-pocket garden.

When a first-year echium came to us in a one-gallon pot, I planted it out in the vegetable patch. Over the course of the summer its rosette of narrow leaves expanded consid-erably, atop a woody stem. In autumn I transplanted it into a five-gallon pot and lugged it downhill into the unheated greenhouse. The plant sulked miserably for a while but picked up over winter. The following spring, as the green-house heated up, I almost drowned the echium with over-watering before getting it planted back out in the garden. For weeks it teetered on the brink of death, its leaves drooping dispiritedly. But again it rallied and bulked up over the summer. Repotting and dragging it back into the greenhouse once more in autumn, I realized with horror that I was turning into my father, a zealot who trundled enormous potted plants indoors every fall to elude Ontario's killing winters. As a boy I'd considered him mad. Now here I was, doing precisely the same thing.

In its third year, I dragged the big echium back out again, wobbled it uphill in the wheelbarrow, and replanted it for a final time. It produced a flowering spike about seven feet tall, its length massed with hundreds of small, lavender-blue flowers. A gorgeous tower of jewels, entirely worth the bother. And then it died. Its babies died, too. British Columbia's Gulf Islands are no more the Canary Islands than they are the Galapagos Islands.

Brash humans may imagine that they have sole con-trol over what grows where in their gardens, but plants, in their Darwinian struggle for dominance, clearly have other ideas. From the plant's point of view, we are really just "the help." Extremists among us—and generally it's a good thing to have extremists in a field—consider plants fully sentient and conscious. We converse with our plants on a regular basis, offering words of encouragement when the impetus to growth has slackened, apologizing for unkind pruning cuts or inept transplanting, perhaps delivering a tongue lashing to chronic underachievers. If we concede that plants are sentient beings, then it's no tall step to accept that they have highly sophisticated survival strategies in which we gardeners may unwittingly play a part.

Vines are a notoriously unruly group, as Darwin himself acknowledged in his 1875 book, *The Movements and Habits of Climbing Plants*. Sandy and I have a couple of golden hops, *Humulus lupulus* Aureus, that could break your heart with their beauty when they shine in the westering sun of a June late afternoon. But tell them where and how to grow? Forget it. The hops throw their twining arms in all directions, indifferent to calculated growth patterns. They keep a gardener on staff primarily to provide them with structures upon which they can clamber. Likewise, summer jasmine can border on outright insurrection in its refusal to accept direction. Perennial loose-limbed slackers such as blue anchusa and Oriental poppies flop down like sulky teenagers on a couch, daring you to say anything. You know full well that you're being used, but there's not a damn thing you can do about it.

I once engaged in an extended bout of Greco-Roman wrestling with a *Clematis montana*, which, after several years as a peaceable, well-balanced Queen of the Vines, suddenly went berserk and began strangling a nearby clump of fountain bamboo. A spasmodic insurrection of this kind is not unlike what glandular teenagers experience—a sudden explosion of growth accompanied by peculiar changes in behavior and appearance. Growth spurts, in my opinion, offer convincing evidence that plants possess both intelligence and a highly refined sense of mischief. Manuals that describe all plants as fast, moderate, or slow-growing to a specified height and width should be read, if at all, as fiction.

Some plants give endless promise of a growth pattern that never happens. For many years now Sandy and I have coddled a Constance Spry rose that could still easily pass for a miniature. She's supposed to be a robust and long-limbed beauty, though, so we've given her a wide berth, never planting other things too close lest they be trampled in the great eruption of growth dear Constance is destined to achieve one of these days. She never has, and never may, unless we were to plant other things close by, which would almost certainly spur her into action. In such instances the challenge is for the gardener to distinguish between a long-delayed growth spurt and a plant pathologically disinclined to grow at all.

A premature performer can inflict even greater heartache. One of our earliest acquisitions was a little tamarisk tree. We'd scarcely put it in the ground when it threw up a beautiful big leader and soon bloomed a somewhat questionable pink. This initial growth spurt was the tree's last, and thereafter the tamarisk settled, rather grumpily, into a routine of neither growing up nor dying down very much. A variation on this theme is the intermittent growth spurt, whereby a plant will explode into lush and profuse growth one year, but not the next—maybe not again until you've decided it won't. Such random patterning is especially embarrassing with plants that require staking or structures to climb over. After the first big burst, you erect a trellis or arbor or obelisk to hold the monster up; the following year it decides not to grow at all, leaving your construction looming over the garden like a fool's delusion of grandeur. Failure to install proper retaining structures, on the other hand, guarantees that the plant will run amok.

There's no end of variations in the growth-spurt game. There's the semi-spurt, for example, whenever things are getting dull. A plant that is developing at a decent pace into a comely shape will suddenly, for no apparent reason, undergo a growth spurt in only one branch. One of our crab apples pulled this stunt, undermining the symmetry of a carefully pruned crown by sticking a single, skinny arm up into the sky, like the class goody-two-shoes who always knows the answer. This tendency can turn a bit ugly in what I call the kinky growth spurt; here again you get a singular burst of growth but in a perverse direction. One of our silver maples insisted on extending a long arm out sideways, as though pointing at us accusingly over some imagined insult.

Some plants, too, exhibit an almost malicious low cunning. Take the imitators. These interlopers situate themselves among plants to which they bear a resemblance, hoping to escape detection. Creeping buttercup is always trying this trick among our strawberries. Trailing blackberry—that thug among the soft fruits—slips furtively into the raspberry patch and sets about its heinous work.

It's as plain as daisies that plants communicate among themselves, constantly making trade-offs about who gets to grow where, how the available sunshine and moisture are to be divvied up and, like certain quarrelsome couples, who's supporting whom and for how long. Sometimes it feels as though the garden is an enormous exchange in which deals are being brokered, compromises made, old enmities nurtured. Only a naif would fail to realize that the gardener's labor is one of the commodities being bartered. Do plants consider us poseurs for taking so much credit for their strength and beauty? I suspect some of the regal lilies look upon me with contempt, and I've been snubbed dreadfully by Himalayan blue poppies. The responsibilities of running a garden are sufficiently onerous, it seems to me, without the added complication of having to worry about what evolutionary strategies our plants may be covertly developing. In the end—difficult as this is to contemplate—they may actually be smarter than we are.

I'm reminded of what I've been reduced to most graphically by the cunning ruses of rhubarb. In thirty years of trying, I had never raised a rhubarb crop that wasn't pathetic. Limp little stems. Dyspeptic leaves. Premature outbreaks of runty flowering stems. An accomplished rhubarbarian might have diagnosed chronic nitrogen deficiency. I chose to blame defective roots, tearing out old ones and replacing them with new. I blamed the inhospitable site and moved the patch from place to place. I blamed lack of moisture and set trickling hoses at the roots. Each spring I piled on inordinate amounts of compost. Nothing helped.

Then, an epiphany. Sandy was listening to her favorite gardening guru on the radio—something she does with a rapt attentiveness seldom evident during any of my own pronouncements—when a caller described a rhubarb performance identical to ours. Nitrogen, the expert advised, nitrogen, nitrogen, nitrogen. Shortly thereafter a moment of pure genius dawned: we decided to try pouring urine on the plants.

The capturing and distribution of human urine is not a subject discussed in polite society. You can thumb through a hundred garden manuals and not find a single reference to the topic. An old English encyclopedia titled *The Garden for Expert and Amateur,* edited by E.T. Ellis, is refreshingly forthcoming on the topic. "Gardeners do not realise as they ought to the immense value of human urine in the garden," the old book states without blushing. "In the limited cases where urine is used, it is the truth to say it is used in the wrong way. Instead of the gardener making arrangements with the servants to save the urine and keep it separately for him, he goes down to the cesspool and pumps the liquid up to the garden again...Soap suds and human urine are not a good mixture, and frequently turn the soil sour...The gardener should arrange that all urine made in the children's nurseries and in the bedrooms be saved for him, and emptied into one of three barrels daily during the summer months." After having fermented in the barrels for at least several days, the urine is ready for use.

The author was recommending a urine collection regime gratifyingly like the one we've employed at our place for years. The precise mechanics I shall leave to your imagination, except to note that the tasks previously performed by the servants and the gardener have fallen to me. At first we used our stored urine primarily to activate compost heaps, but lately I had taken to pouring it directly around the roots of certain trees and shrubs. (This operation, being more noble in conception than in execution, must be conducted with utmost discretion, preferably when no visitors are expected.)

"When required for use," our encyclopedia continues, "a can should be dipped into one of the barrels and this should be filled about one-fifth of its capacity with the fermented urine. The can is then filled up with water. This is, generally speaking, a safe liquid manure for strong-growing crops, but as the strength of human urine is apt to vary somewhat according to diet, health condition of its producer, and period of its passage, it is well to test the diluted liquid first by pouring some over the foliage of large-leaved weeds." I had first-hand experience of this potency when, in pouring undiluted urine around the roots of a boxwood hedge, I accidentally splashed the silvery leaves of some nearby snow-in-summer. Within days the little ground cover's leaves were as scorched as though they'd been blasted with Agent Orange.

Throughout late winter and early spring, I trudged up to the vegetable patch carrying full twin buckets and poured the magic liquid around the roots of the emerging rhubarb. They gulped it down. And then a miracle occurred, as stirring as any at Lourdes or Fatima. Lusty new shoots sprang forth. Enormous leaves unfurled. Our rhubarb runts were transformed into brutes, like baseball players on steroids. Nary a flowering stem emerged for months. Years of debilitating failure slipped away. I felt redeemed, reborn. The boost of such a triumph allowed me to sail blithely above jests of questionable taste concerning our rhubarb pies.

But here's the rub: the patch has become too productive. There's only so much stewed rhubarb and rhubarb pie two people can consume. The rest goes into barrels of rhubarb wine. Fermented in the greenhouse during the glorious warmth of summer, the wine runneth over. And over. We guzzle the stuff all winter and spring, like camels at an oasis. Which naturally leads to an increased frequency and fulsomeness of peeing. Which in turn provides an ever more ample supply of fermented urine, which, when applied to the rhubarb bed, ensures an even more abundant crop. You can see where this is going. I've diverted some of the urine elsewhere, but nevertheless we're producing enough rhubarb wine to float a houseboat.

It's an ignominious end, really, leaving me to ponder how *Homo sapiens* has evolved, in starkest Darwinian terms, into an organism whose primary function is to deliver its urine to demanding, undeniably more highly evolved life forms.

Down the
Garden Pathology

THERE IS AT the heart of all fine gardening a sublime ascent from dirt to the heavens. "In the assemblies of the enlightened ones," wrote Zen grand master Dogen Zenji, "there have been many cases of mastering the Way bringing forth the heart of plants and trees; this is what awakening the mind for enlightenment is like." It is an experience we long for, a state of consciousness we dream about. And yet, for all our meditations, we repeatedly find that we are stuck in the mud. Earthbound. Dug in.

But why? What holds us down? Perhaps before undertaking any spiritual flights of fancy, any lifting of our eyes to the stars, we need first to take a therapeutic stroll down the garden pathology. To stare, if you will, unflinchingly into the dirt to examine those components of the psyche that inhibit our longed-for transcendence. This is a journey not for the faint of heart nor for the readily offended, for it requires that we look steadfastly at the ghouls and monsters lurking beneath the surface of even the most immaculate of gardens.

Let us commence gently with a common affliction, the chronic moving of plants from place to place. To the novice gardener, the business of shifting plants may seem a perilous thing, to be undertaken only for the most pressing reasons. Trembling with misgivings, the novice excavates a root-ball the size of Liechtenstein and sprints with it to the new planting hole fleeter than Perdita Felicien. But pretty soon one gets the hang of moving plants around. Over time one becomes increasingly nonchalant about deciding to lift and relocate a certain shrub or vine for the greater good of the whole. This state of equanimity is a happy middle ground between the trepidations of the past and the follies that lie ahead. We may even deceive ourselves into believing that we are beginning to master the Way.

But follies follow, sure as slugs after showers. Gradually, imperceptibly, transplanting starts to take on a life of its own. The gardener begins prowling the grounds less to bring forth the heart of plants and trees and more to locate something that might need moving. You find people digging up perfectly well-situated specimens and replanting them elsewhere for no reason other than that they feel so much better when they're able to move something. Anything.

Size is no deterrent, either. For some of these fixated souls, the bigger the movable object the better. You see them appraisingly eying a tree in their yard, an impossibly large tree, a tree that is appropriate just as it is. But no. "That tree is preposterous there," they announce. The hearts of other family members sink as they foresee weeks of bedlam dominated by excavating, moving, and replanting. Admittedly, one distinct advantage of being a compulsive mover is that you don't need to squander time deciding where to replant whatever is being moved, because it's sure to be moved again in short order. Locating things in their proper place is not the point of the exercise.

If there's nothing at hand that can possibly be moved, the gardener starts to get jittery. Unable to control herself, she bursts outdoors and engages in highly stylized moving gestures, much like tai chi, that you sincerely hope the neighbors aren't observing. In such a case, it is preferable that innocent bystanders suggest a plant be moved, any plant, to calm the jangled sufferer. Otherwise, the shaky gardener is apt to insist upon the grandest gesture of all: abandoning the house and moving someplace else. Other members of the household will be responsible for transporting furniture, clothing, and housewares to the new location, while the gardener is busy transporting the entire garden, leaving behind a yard pockmarked with holes like craters on the moon.

The chronic moving of plants is just one of a battery of obsessive-compulsive disorders that may beset the gardener. This kind of disorder is particularly prevalent, because so many plantspeople are confirmed creatures of ritual. Obsessive counting, for example. When you're planting beans or peas or corn you can't stop yourself from counting the seeds: one, two, three, four. You drop each counted seed into the ground—one, two, three, four. You never arrive at a grand total, and it would make no difference if you did. You have no idea why you're counting each spadeful of compost you're dumping into the wheelbarrow; you just are. You may try whistling or singing or recalling a clever conversation from the evening before, but the ritualized counting continues.

Examine almost any potting shed and you'll see abundant evidence of another obsessive behavior: compulsive hoarding. Thousands of pieces of twine knotted uselessly together in a box. Hundreds of identification tags for plants that disappeared decades ago. Ancient spade blades and rake tines, lacking handles. Seed packets dating back to the Middle Ages. Stacks and stacks of plastic pots and planting trays.

Certain other gardeners become obsessed with a particular species or genera. They have a dahlia phase, during which nothing but a dahlia will do. They join the local dahlia society, enter their prized specimens in dahlia shows, dally over dahlias anywhere. Eventually wearying, they plunge into an iris phase instead. Successive genera fixations lead to the yard being in a perpetual state of turmoil.

Another all too common affliction is the horticultural inferiority complex. In its advanced forms, this goes far beyond the commonplace feeling that one's garden isn't up to snuff. Rather than the dog's breakfast you fear it to be, your garden is transformed in imagination into a pleasure ground of unimaginable beauty. Like a horticultural Walter Mitty, you fantasize yourself admired far and wide for your accomplishments. International celebrities drop by to admire your hemerocallis collection. Brad Pitt whispers breathily in your ear that he's lost his heart to your *Cardiospermum halicacabum*. David Beckham confesses coyly that he'd love to bend wisteria tendrils with you. On and on the inferiority-complexed gardener goes, entertaining increasingly elaborate fantasies while giving the outward appearance of being the most unassuming of persons.

Unlike the poor eccentric specimen next door, who suffers from another unfortunate horticultural condition: extreme introversion. The guy never talks to anyone except himself and his plants. He never goes anywhere except into his garden. He spends most of his waking hours installing chain-link fences and wrought iron gates. His notion of a healthy sex life is to fondle his Brussels sprouts and stroke his rhubarb shoots. Left too long alone, he's plagued by irrational prejudices and paranoid fantasies. He suspects that if he grows Neapolitan parsley or spaghetti squash, he'll start gesturing extravagantly with his hands. He's convinced that bok choy and gai lan are components of a Chinese plot to take over the world. He's a great believer in oracles and prophecies and is easily hoodwinked by charlatans. So he'll order the latest whiz-bang gardening tool advertised on late-night television— perhaps a pair of loppers whose telescoping handles can be twisted backward to form a multi-grip pipe wrench.

Ah, he's a sad little chap, this horticultural hermit, and we can have a good laugh at his expense. But his disorder is no worse than that equally insidious condition that afflicts so many gardeners: the horticultural version of generalized anxiety disorder. This is a state of the mind marked by a pervasive unease that things are bound to go terribly wrong. It's not a fear of one specific thing, like arachnophobia, but a diffuse anxiety that disaster of some generalized sort awaits us. The symptoms are manifold. Take the simple matter of seeds, for example. There's no end of worrying one can do over seeds. Perhaps they haven't arrived yet, provoking a fear that you put your order in too late, that the seed house is bankrupt, that your package is lost in the strife-ridden bowels of the post office. When the seeds do arrive, you switch over to worrying that you ordered the wrong varieties or that you didn't order enough. Planting can become an orgy of anxiety. Is it too early? Too late? Why haven't they germinated yet? Have I watered them too much? Too little, perhaps? Is my starting mix all right? Your condition worsening by the day, you begin practicing strange fetishistic rituals, frequently involving a mister. Finally the little pipsqueaks poke their noses above ground and you begin fretting about damping-off.

But all of these worries are mere preliminaries to the full anxiety onslaught. Not content with worrying about a flat of insignificant seedlings, the gardener works his stress up to a grand operatic pitch: "Holy moly, I can't sleep at night, I'm so wired. I lie awake for hours worrying about whether my soil pH is right. Am I watering the dianthus too heavily? Have I been a fool with the gooseberries? It's awful, you know. I'll be out there pruning the clematis—are those the ones you're supposed to cut all the way back or only lightly prune? I can never remember—when suddenly I become light-headed. I can't seem to focus; my arm's gone numb. Oh my God, I'm having a heart attack! It's true, I've been pushing myself too hard lately. I should've sold this place years ago and brought a condo, but it'd be just my luck to get a leaky condo. I'm probably better off here. Except my ankles and knees are killing me. Could this be the onset of osteoporosis? I've got to get up on the ladder and prune those damn watershoots out of the plum tree, though I'll probably fall off and smack my head on the sidewalk and have to lie in a vegetative state in some hospital corridor while my family argues about whether or not to remove my life support system. But at least I won't be pounding around in this confounded garden, with the headaches and sweating and trembling. It's too much! It's all too much! Excuse me, please, I've got to go lie down and take a Valium."

Gardeners, of course, love to specialize. Many, not content to be limited to a general anxiety disorder, cultivate a particular variety of stress disorder. Social anxiety disorder, for example. This is a phobia in which the sufferer becomes intensely self-conscious in social situations. You think you're being observed by other people and judged unfavorably. You feel inadequate, incompetent, humiliated. But the truth of the matter is you *are* being observed by other people and judged by them. What else would you expect, wearing your muddy boots and your battered old trousers with dirt patches on the knees, and a shirt no thrift store would lower itself to sell? You're being scrutinized by others because you look like something out of the 1932 *Farmer's Almanac*. There you are in some hideously overpriced bistro with the smart set all gabbing away about what's new and thrilling on the runways of Paris and Milan, what extravagances Liz Claiborne has concocted, and how daring Karl Lagerfeld has been in his new designs. But all you can think of to add to the conversation is your news of that enormous centipede you encountered in your compost pile yesterday. I mean, what gardener wouldn't have a social anxiety disorder?

Or a panic disorder, for that matter. You know, that incredible assault on your nervous system that comes when you feel you've totally lost control. Your heart's racing and pounding; you can hear it in there thumping like a mating grouse. You can't breathe, you're pouring sweat, you're dizzy, you feel as if you might faint at any second. Ninety-nine times out of a hundred, a horticultural panic attack occurs when your total bill has been rung up at your favorite nursery. Arrrgggh!!! You stagger home with an enormous load of plant material that you have no room for in your garden, knowing full well that your loving companion is going to go ballistic when he discovers what you've done on the credit card. And you know you've just set yourself up for a lengthy bout of post-traumatic stress disorder. Years later, you'll be jolted awake in the middle of the night, haunted by the disturbing remembrance of having spent several months' salary for a new magnolia cultivar, which died several days after the little nursery you bought it from was driven out of business by the cut-rate nursery stock at supersized box stores.

Other gardeners fall victim to the class of pathologies known as mood disorders. There are two types of these: unipolar and bipolar. The first we commonly call depression, and there are few sights more heart-wrenching than a gardener embedded in full-blown floral depression.

"Ah, cripes, I don't know. Just look at this bloody dump. I've tried my best here, I really have. But it's all wrong. No, no! Don't try to sweet-talk me out of it. It's a disaster. That liquidambar—it shouldn't be where it is. You know it; I know it; the liquidambar knows it. But it's too big to move. I guess I should cut it down and burn it. Great. I thought I'd at least got the bones of this garden right, but you know, I've seen jellyfish on the beach with better bones than this mess. That pathetic patch of salvia over there—thought it would add a welcome splash of color. 'Blazing torches' they call it, or something like that. It looks like psychedelic dog vomit. Ah, you keep trying. You bring in some sanguisorbas and a few new euphorbias and a chocolate eupatorium. Phfff! No matter what you do, the place keeps looking worse each year. It's bad karma, man, you know what I mean? There're weeds crawling over everything. Your favorite plants keep dying on you because the water's full of chlorine and the air's so polluted you need a gas mask to breathe. And the hole in the ozone. And the greenhouse effect. And the oil cartel running the world. I mean, really, what's the goddamn point of any of it anymore?"

With bipolar mood disorder, the depression cycles with periods of mania. Suddenly, everything's fun. Motivation surges. The gardener feels a tremendous empowerment. The mood is one of explosive euphoria. Out he charges into the garden, determined to tear out all this pseudo-romantic English, pastel-colored claptrap—it's *so* yesterday—and replace the entire thing with a Mediterranean garden. Trees crash down, bonfires roar, trash bins bulge with refuse, dirt flies, Stonehenge-sized stones are bullied into position. "Look at this! Just look at what's happening! I'm going to have a flight of stone steps over there," his arm sweeps majestically uphill, "agaves in huge pots all along the terrace, a grove of cordyline palms where that ludicrous liquidambar used to be. I'm repainting the whole house in sand with sage trim. God, it's gonna be so great! Can you just picture it? I mean, can you?"

Well, actually, no, you can't. And that's because the tearing-down phase invariably outlasts the manic phase. When the font of euphoria runs dry, the freshly depressed gardener is left staring at a sea of rubble. "Oh, God, what a disaster. I mean, really, what's the friggin' use of even trying, eh?"

Of all the pathologies rampant in the gardening community, perhaps the most widespread are phobic disorders: irrational fears, terrors, or aversions, frequently of a morbid character. Step into almost any garden, and you'll discover more phobias crawling around than ground beetles. Some of them are to be expected when encountering a gardener—ablutophobia, for example. The fear of washing or bathing. Especially hands. Never shake hands with a gardener unless you need an extra pound of topsoil. And the fear of washing often extends to clothing. Some gardeners I could name have enough soil on their coveralls to raise a crop of potatoes. Many of the great unwashed attempt to camouflage their affliction by telling you they're organic growers.

On the opposite end of the spectrum are those gardeners who suffer from automysophobia, the fear of being dirty. These people are always dressed in prim gardening outfits with perfectly clean gloves. Their trim and tidy gardens have less bacteria in them than the average hospital operating room (admittedly, that's not saying all that much). Oh, they seem to be the picture of contentment, tripping about with their triple-sanitized trowels and weeding forks, but in reality these neatniks are a seething cauldron of aversions. They're beset by blennophobia, the fear of slime, and spend long hours plotting the annihilation of slugs and snails. They're racked with seplophobia, the fear of decaying matter, and own several nuclear-powered leaf blowers to blast away rotting leaves. They suffer from coprophobia, too, the dread of fecal matter. A splotch of slug excrement on a hosta leaf sends them retching to the toilet. Many of these automysophobes end up as hydroponic growers in sealed chambers where neither soil nor microorganism is permitted.

And maybe that's the smartest way to go, because hydroponic gardening has the considerable advantage of getting you out of the elements, those capricious forces of nature that can trigger a rash of phobias. Like cryophobia, the fear of extreme cold, ice, or frost. Irrationally, you decide to fill your garden with half-hardy and semitropical plants, thereby condemning yourself to spend much of the year wrapping your banana trees and Norfolk Island pines in pink insulation and plastic sheeting, so that the garden resembles the bowels of a Stalinist refrigeration facility. You spend all day listening to weather forecasts and studying your barometer, so that you can dash out in the dark to throw old blankets over your darlings before sudden killing frosts descend. Not surprisingly, most cryophobic gardeners have fled to temperate areas from frigid regions of the country.

But hold your tears, I beseech you, until you consider the terrors of pluviophobia, the fear of rain or of being rained on. "Oh, God, will this confounded downpour never end! The garden's a soggy mess, the peony tips have turned black again, and the peach tree leaves are crumpling with peach leaf curl. The roses are balling up and the lavenders are drowning. Stop raining! Stop bloody raining!" The pluviophobic gardener crouches in his potting shed shaking his fist at the skies.

But eventually the storm abates, skies clear, the sun breaks through the clouds. You bound outdoors enthusiastically but are instantly hit with a wallop of thermophobia, your fear of heat. Horribly, you feel the first twinges of heliophobia, fear of the sun. Your plants begin to cower beneath the relentlessly warming rays. By now you're sweating and twitching uncontrollably in a bout of phengophobia, dread of daylight or sunshine. You take to gardening at four in the morning and nine in the evening, like a desert creature hiding under its rock during the blast-furnace heat of the day. You stumble around in the dusk trundling soaker hoses, trying to stave off both desiccation and xerophobia, the fear of dryness. This is the very condition that leads so many well-meaning people to systematically drown their houseplants.

Amid this grievous suffering, not surprisingly, some gardeners become convinced that nature is not keeping up her part of the bargain. That she is less a partner in the great undertaking of making a garden than a cunning adversary. As this conviction takes hold, you start seeing other living things not as allies but as agents of the enemy. After the deer have stripped your roses and the raccoons have destroyed your corn and the possums have taken your peaches and the rabbits have girdled your apple trees and the voles have stolen your carrots, who wouldn't feel a touch of zoophobia, the fear of animals? Not to mention muriphobia, the dread of mice, especially after they've found their way into your mouse-proof apple storage bins, gnawed indiscriminately, and defecated the same way. A couple of seasons with thieving robins and tree-killing sapsuckers and apple-pecking pileated woodpeckers is more than enough to justify a case of ornithophobia, the fear of birds. A few episodes of harvesting ripe peaches and plums and getting viciously stung by the winged insects hiding inside the splitting fruit is more than sufficient to trigger a bout of spheksophobia, the fear of wasps. Myrmecophobia, the fear of ants, is entirely justified by their foul aphid farms on your favorite edibles and ornamentals. Perhaps the most efficient way of proceeding with respect to insects is to lump them together under general entomophobia, the fear of insects. The phobic gardener's shed bulges with so many poisons and chemical weapons of mass destruction, George W. Bush could easily justify an armed invasion in the cause of Peace. And Freedom. And Democracy.

Speaking of Bush and the weaponization of space, what about all those spatial phobias gardeners suffer from? There's megalophobia, for example, the fear of large things. This is a speciality of the rock and alpine plants crowd, who have no use for any plant big enough to be seen without a magnifying glass. And a touch of megalophobia helps enormously if you're into bonsai and determined to have your pine trees remain forever only eight inches tall— which is a debilitating nightmare to anyone afflicted with microphobia, fear of small things. For these big thinkers, a successful city garden is one with five giant sequoias growing on a tiny lot and looming over the neighborhood.

Microphobes are closely aligned with gardeners suffering from kenophobia, the dread of voids or empty spaces.

Kenophobes pack plants into their beds like commuters into Tokyo subway trains. You can't get down their paths without a machete. There's not the tiniest gap to be seen in their startling jungle. If a bit of space does open up, they dash to the greenhouse, grab a filler plant, and jam it into the gap. Which is completely the opposite of people suffering from clithrophobia, the fear of being enclosed. These cowboys love their wide open spaces. So they've got lawns spreading from lot line to lot line and spend most of their waking hours roaring around on their rider mowers and shouting things like "Howdy, partner!" to innocent passersby while singing "Don't Fence Me In." It's a mystery to everyone in the neighborhood why these folks don't pack up and move to the Great Plains, except maybe they've just moved *from* the Great Plains and are determined to drag a piece of it along with them.

These people are not all that different from gardeners who suffer with asymmetriphobia, the fear of asymmetrical things. Asymmetriphobic gardens are all straight lines, clipped hedges, precisely matching topiaries, rows of fastigiate trees lined up like marines at boot camp. No path is permitted to curve, no shrub to sprawl, no tree to weep. Order! Discipline! Control! Trouble is, it's impossible to be in one of these gardens without being distracted, one's better self notwithstanding, by rude speculations concerning the owner's early childhood toilet training. But, then again, are they any more pitiable than their opposites, the gardens of people afflicted with symmetriphobia, the fear

of symmetry? Here there's no order at all. Plants tumble
and crawl over one another like maggots. Paths weave
around as crazily as drunks on Saturday night. As often
as not, the owner also suffers from technophobia, the fear
of technology. "No, I don't like having machines on the
place," he tells you. "I manage quite nicely with my trusty
old hand tools." As he's telling you this, several enormous
kiwi vines grab him by the throat and strangle him.

Color phobias are a whole other affliction. Xanthopho-
bia's the fear of the color yellow and porphyrophobia of
purple. Now, it could be convincingly argued that a dash
of aversion to yellow and purple is something certain gardens would benefit from. Unhappily, people afflicted this
way are frequently driven into the folly of creating a white
garden. I call this the Sissinghurst seduction. Compe-
tently done, a white garden can be a thing of considerable
charm; improperly done, an unfortunate display of floricultural anemia.

There are any number of other phobias we gardeners
entertain for perfectly valid reasons. Almost all of us have
thaasophobia, for example, the fear of sitting. Why would
you ever want to sit down when you could be digging
something somewhere? Or the closely related hedonopho-
bia, terror of feeling pleasure. For one thing, how can you
possibly be feeling pleasure when your decidophobia, the
fear of making decisions, is acting up?

"Darling, do you think that willow-leafed sunflower
would look best over here beside the Japanese anemones,

or would it be better over there where it can play against the *Cimicifuga racemosa?*"

"Gee, I dunno. Maybe here. No, no! Maybe it's best with the cimicifuga."

"Hmm. But won't it get lost over there so close to the contorted willow foliage, which is really very similar?"

"Yes, you've got a point there. Maybe we should put it by the Japanese anemones."

"Well, perhaps, but you know the anenomes show to best effect without any intruding clutter."

"True enough, darling. Well, what shall we do?"

"I dunno."

"I don't either."

"Hmmm."

On it goes for hours, days, weeks as decidophobic gardeners stand immobilized. Perhaps part of the problem is a hint of catagelophobia, the fear of being ridiculed. "Is someone laughing at my ligularia?" We are artists, after all, and it's entirely reasonable that we might tremble before a cruel world's judgment of our artistry.

Certain gardeners have crossed the frontier of phobic decency when it comes to plant-based fears. You might accept a case of alliumphobia, the fear of garlic, as an unfortunate but understandable affliction. Or mycophobia, an aversion to mushrooms. Even dendrophobia, the fear of trees. But it really is pushing the envelope to have so many gardens blatantly proclaiming their owners' lachano-phobia, the fear of vegetables. They'll have every conceivable ornamental from all corners of the globe, the mass of them blooming away and flaunting their foliage and teasing with textures and forms, but not a single beanstalk to be seen. No spinach. No corn. No row of robust rutabagas. I mean, what are these people thinking? Veteran vegetable cultivators retaliate with anthrophobia, the fear of flowers. They'd as soon die as see a skanky scabiosa disporting itself amid their vegetables.

Most pathetic of all among growers are those condemned to a life of botanophobia, the fear of plants. They have nothing at all growing in their yards. But their patios are paved in brilliant Moroccan tiles. They've got enormous painted pots from Senegal and marvelous urns and sundials and classical statuary and postmodernist sculptures fashioned from recycled plumbing fixtures. And they love to talk about "our *garden*" and how it won top prize for finest garden in the city and was photographed for home and garden magazines and appeared on television, even though there's not a single living thing in it.

But you know, in the end it doesn't matter whether you've got vegetables or not or flowers or not, or even plants or not. Because there's a rogue's gallery of other phobias that invariably bring us all low. I'm talking about the terror of physical ailments. It might start with something as simple as a little bout of acrophobia, the fear of drafts or airborne noxious substances, then move on to pathophobia, the fear of disease. Suddenly, you get a disconcerting attack of ponophobia, the dread of overworking

or of pain. This leads to kyphophobia, the fear of stoop-
ing—the awful sensation that if you bend over to do some
weeding you may never get straight again. Or generalized
ankylophobia, fear of immobility of a joint, a reasonable
anxiety when you consider the number of gardeners with
elbows that don't bend as they used to and knees and hips
that don't work so good anymore. Sometimes you feel you
could easily convene your garden club meetings in the
waiting line for joint replacement surgery. Understand-
ably, you become terrorized by dystychiphobia, a dread of
accidents, and—fatal for the well-ordered garden—ergo-
phobia, the fear of work. Dementophobia comes next, the
fear of insanity. This may be the best-founded of the horticultural phobias. Or perhaps that honor belongs to the
last in this sad category, gerascophobia, dread of growing
old. You can't possibly go getting old with all that work still
left to do.

Is it any wonder, then, that so many gardeners tumble
like harvested potatoes into the bottomless hopper of dis-
sociative disorders? Our identities become fragmented.
We lose our selves. We begin by forgetting things. Now
where did I leave that bloody rake? Hey, has anybody
seen my work gloves? These are the first alarming hints
of what will grow into psychogenic amnesia. Plant names
tiptoe out of memory, never to return. You spend whole
afternoons staring pitiably at an *Ampelopsis brevipedun-
culata,* trying to remember what the hell it's called. People's names go next. You see old what's-his-name down the
street out fussing as usual with his wretched persicarias,

and though you've known him for twenty-five years you can't for the life of you remember his name. Everyone you run into on the street or in the shops looks vaguely familiar. Is that person glancing at you your old pal Charley, or is he a stranger? You can't tell. "Oh, hi!" you're prepared to say enthusiastically to everybody you encounter, just to cover the bases. Most embarrassing of all, you forget who *you* are. You look in the mirror one morning and a perfect stranger stares back at you. This is why so many gardeners succumb to a fugue state. They find themselves one day in a strange locale far from home, unable to recall how they got there or what they're doing there or whom they're doing it with. It almost certainly isn't gardening.

At its most extreme, dissociation hurtles some gardeners into the bizarre world of multiple personality disorder. The Dr. Jekyll and Mr. Hyde thing. Under normal circumstances these are the most amiable and enjoyable of companions, but get them anywhere near a garden and they mutate into monsters.

"Just look at that veronicastrum," the horticultural Mr. Hyde sneers. "Perfectly hideous. And that *Parthenocissus henryana* should be permanently banned from cultivation."

Trying to lighten the mood, you point out an ornamental grass. "Isn't that an attractive miscanthus?" you say.

"That's not a miscanthus," he snaps, "that's a *Spodiopogon sibiricus*. Any damn fool would know that."

Taken together, these various neuroses, psychoses, phobias, and mood disorders congeal into chronic hortophobia, a disease that undermines one's very faith in oneself as a gardener. The garden's all wrong, you conclude, completely, irretrievably wrong. You doubt the integrity of its design, your ability to improve it, your relationship with plants, your fitness to even call yourself a gardener. It's been said that the difference between failure and success is doing a thing nearly right and doing it exactly right. You have come to the appalling conclusion that your garden is not now, nor ever will be, exactly right. You're assailed by the conviction that you're fundamentally incompetent, that you have been fooling yourself with ridiculous pretensions. Your insatiable passion is exposed as pathetic illusion. You have reached the nadir of your gardening career. It is from this dark place that you must begin the long climb back toward the light of self-respect, employing the wisdom that sprouts only in the gloom of despair.

Horticultural therapists tell us that the first crucial step to recovery involves an open confession of your plight. There is no need for concealment; you have nothing left to hide. You speak to your fears and failures honestly. In doing so, you discover a wonderful thing: that you are not alone, that others have suffered through this same debilitating experience and emerged from it stronger than before. There are painful steps still to take, of course, steps in which you'll work your way through denial, blame, and anger. No matter: you have begun. The dam is burst. Tears flow at this point. Much hugging ensues. Your family and friends rally around you. You're the comeback kid, ready to once again fearlessly fathom the depths of passion. This is what awakening the mind for enlightenment is like.

DES KENNEDY has lived for the past thirty-five years with his partner, Sandy, in their hand-hewn home on one of British Columbia's Gulf Islands. The author of countless magazine pieces and five previous books—two novels and three collections of essays—Kennedy has also made numerous TV and radio appearances and written for and narrated documentary films. A popular speaker on the gardening circuit, Kennedy has been active in the environmental scene for many years and was a founding director of a community land trust on his home island.